Colonial America Biographies

Colonial
America
Biographies

Volume 2:
M-Z

PEGGY SAARI
Julie Carnagie, Editor

AN IMPRINT OF THE GALE GROUP

DETROIT · SAN FRANCISCO · LONDON
BOSTON · WOODBRIDGE, CT

Peggy Saari

Staff

Julie L. Carnagie, *U•X•L Editor*
Carol DeKane Nagel, *U•X•L Managing Editor*
Thomas L. Romig, *U•X•L Publisher*

Shalice Shah-Caldwell, *Permissions Associate (Pictures)*

Rita Wimberley, *Senior Buyer*
Evi Seoud, *Assistant Production Manager*
Dorothy Maki, *Manufacturing Manager*

Pamela A. E. Galbreath, *Senior Art Director*
Cynthia Baldwin, *Product Design Manager*

LM Design, *Typesetting*

Library of Congress Cataloging-in-Publication Data

Saari, Peggy.
  Colonial America : biographies / Peggy Saari : Julie L. Carnagie, editor.
    p. cm.
  Includes bibliographical references and indexes.
    Contents: v. 1. A-L — v. 2. M-Z.
  Summary: Profiles sixty men and women from the American colonial era, including explorers, founders of colonies, religious leaders, landowners, artists, and more.
  ISBN 0-7876-3760-2 (set). — ISBN   0-7876-3761-0 (v. 1). — ISBN 0-7876-3762-9 (v. 2)
  1. United States—History—Colonial period, ca. 1600-1775 Biography Dictionaries Juvenile literature. [1. United   States—History—Colonial period, ca. 1600-1775 Biography.] I. Carnagie, Julie. II. Title.
  E187.5.S23   1999
  973.2'092'2
  [B]—DC21   99-20707
                                                                       CIP

Cover photographs (top to bottom): Cotton Mather reproduced by permission of the Library of Congress; Anne Marbury Hutchinson reproduced by permission Corbis Corporation (Bellevue); Pontiac reproduced by permission of the city of Pontiac, Michigan.

Printed in the United States of America
10 9 8 7 6 5 4 3 2 1

Contents

Volume 2: M-Z

Advisory Board

Special thanks are due for the invaluable comments and suggestions provided by U•X•L's Colonial America Reference Library advisors:

- Katherine L. Bailey, Library Media Specialist, Seabreeze High School, Daytona Beach, Florida.

- Jonathan Betz-Zall, Children's Librarian, Sno-Isle Regional Library System, Edmonds, Washington.

- Deborah Hammer, Manager of the Social Sciences Division, Queens Borough Public Library, New Hyde Park, New York.

- Fannie Louden, Fifth Grade History Teacher, B. F. Yancey Elementary School, Esmont, Virginia.

Reader's Guide

Colonial America: Biographies presents the biographies of women and men relevant to the colonial era in America. Among the sixty people profiled in each of the two volumes are explorers, Native Americans, and people who helped to found and shape the American colonies. *Colonial America: Biographies* does not only include biographies of readily recognizable figures of the colonial era, such as Italian explorer Christopher Columbus, founder of the Pennsylvania colony William Penn, and banished religious leader Anne Marbury Hutchinson, but it also includes profiles of people such as Margaret Brent, the first woman landowner in Maryland, and John Smibert, the first painter to capture life in the colonies.

Additional features

Colonial America: Biographies also contains short biographies of people who are in some way connected with the main biographee and sidebars highlighting interesting information. More than one hundred black-and-white illustrations enliven the text, while cross-references are made to other people profiled in the two-volume set. Each entry concludes with a list of sources—including web sites—for further information for additional study, and both volumes contain a timeline, a glossary, and a cumulative index of the subjects discussed in *Colonial America: Biographies*.

Comments and suggestions

We welcome your comments on this work as well as your suggestions for topics to be featured in future editions of *Colonial America: Biographies*. Please write: Editors, *Colonial America: Biographies*, U•X•L, 27500 Drake Rd., Farmington Hills, MI 48331-3535; call toll-free: 1-800-877-4253; fax: 248-414-5043; or send e-mail via www.galegroup.com.

Timeline of Events in Colonial America

1492   Italian explorer **Christopher Columbus** opens the way for European settlement of the Americas.

1524   Italian explorer **Giovanni da Verrazano** becomes the first European to sight New York Harbor.

1535   French explorer **Jacques Cartier** discovers the St. Lawrence River.

1538   Spanish conquistador **Francisco Vásquez de Coronado** begins searching for the fabled Seven Cities of Cibola.

1539   Moroccan "medicine man" **Estevanico** is killed by Zuni warriors.

1542   Spanish explorer **Hernando de Soto** leads the first European party to discover the Mississippi River.

1495-97	1517	1534
Leonardo da Vinci paints *The Last Supper*	Martin Luther posts his 95 theses	Henry VIII founds Church of England

1475	1500	1525	1550

1608	Powhatan-Renapé "princess" **Pocahontas** saves Jamestown settlers from starvation.
1609	English navigator **Henry Hudson** discovers the Hudson River, a major waterway in present-day New York State.
1609	Chief **Powhatan** establishes peaceful relations with the Virginia colonists.
1612	French explorer **Samuel de Champlain** founds New France.
1612	Virginia colonist **John Rolfe** perfects a strain of tobacco for export to England.
1614	Former Virginia colonist **John Smith** explores and names New England.
1621	Wampanoag chief **Massasoit** signs a treaty with the Plymouth colonists.
1627	Massachusetts fur trader **Thomas Morton** angers Puritans by building a giant Maypole and celebrating May Day.
1630	Plymouth Colony governor **William Bradford** begins writing *Of Plymouth Plantation*.
1630	Puritan leader **John Winthrop** founds Massachusetts Bay Colony.
1633	Influential Puritan clergyman **John Cotton** moves to the Massachusetts Bay Colony.
1636	Massachusetts Bay Colony leader **John Endecott** initiates the Pequot War.
1638	Religious dissenter **Anne Marbury Hutchinson** is put on trial for heresy.
1639	French missionary **Marie Guyart** moves to New France to start a convent for Native Americans.

1616 William Shakespeare dies	1620 The Mayflower Compact is signed	1625 Fort Amsterdam is founded	1633 Galileo is tried for heresy	1636 Harvard College is founded

1610	1620	1630	1640

1644 Religious and political dissident **Roger Williams** founds Rhode Island.

1646 Dutch military leader **Peter Stuyvesant** is appointed director-general of New Netherlands.

c. 1647 Amateur lawyer **Margaret Brent** unsuccessfully petitions the Maryland assembly for the right to vote.

1650 *The Tenth Muse,* a collection of poems by Massachusetts Puritan poet **Anne Bradstreet**, is published. She is America's first female poet.

1651 Former African slave **Anthony Johnson** owns a 250-acre estate at Pungoteague Creek in Virginia.

1651 Puritan preacher and educator **John Eliot** establishes the first town for "praying Indians."

1660 Quaker dissident **Mary Dyer** is executed by Puritans in Massachusetts.

1670s Puritan minister **Edward Taylor** begins writing poetry expressing his religious beliefs.

1673 French-Canadian explorer **Louis Jolliet** and French missionary **Jacques Marquette** discover the Mississippi River.

1674 New Amsterdam housewife **Maria van Cortlandt van Rensselaer** takes over management of Rensselaerswyck, a large plantation.

1675 Wampanoag chief **Metacom (King Philip)** starts King Philip's War.

1676 Virginia political dissident **Nathaniel Bacon** leads a rebellion against the Franchise Act, which restricts voting rights to a few wealthy landowners.

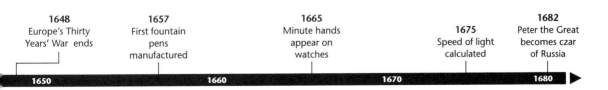

1648
Europe's Thirty
Years' War ends

1657
First fountain
pens
manufactured

1665
Minute hands
appear on
watches

1675
Speed of light
calculated

1682
Peter the Great
becomes czar
of Russia

1650　　　　1660　　　　1670　　　　1680

1676	Connecticut colonist **Mary White Rowlandson** and her children are taken captive by the Wampanoag tribe.
1679	Mohawk holy woman **Catherine (Kateri) Tekakwitha** founds a convent for Native American women.
1680	Pueblo revolutionary leader **Popé** drives the Spanish out of New Mexico.
1682	French explorer **René-Robert Cavelier de La Salle** discovers the mouth of the Mississippi River.
1682	Quaker minister **William Penn** founds Pennsylvania.
1687	Austrian Jesuit missionary **Eusebio Francisco Kino** begins his work in New Mexico.
1689	Calvinist political leader **Jacob Leisler** stages a rebellion against Catholic rule in New York.
1693	Boston clergyman and scientist **Cotton Mather** defends the Salem witch trials.
1697	British privateer **William Kidd** becomes a pirate.
1697	Massachusetts judge **Samuel Sewall** makes a public apology for his role in the Salem witch trials.
1704	Massachusetts businesswoman **Sarah Kemble Knight** writes about her trip through New England to New York City.
1720	Wealthy Virginia landowner and politician **William Byrd II** succeeds in upholding the power of the Council of Virginia.
1730	Boston portrait painter **John Smibert** gains fame as America's first artist.
1733	English social reformer **James Edward Oglethorpe** founds Georgia as a penal colony.

1692
Aesop's Fables
is published

1701
War of Spanish
Succession
begins

1714
War of Spanish
Succession ends

1721
Postal service
between
London and
New England
begins

| 1690 | 1700 | 1710 | 1720 |

1735   The not-guilty verdict in the trial of newspaper publisher **John Peter Zenger** establishes freedom of the press in America.

1739   Evangelical preacher **George Whitefield** sparks the Great Awakening, a series of religious revivals, in the American colonies.

1741   New England minister **Jonathan Edwards** delivers his famous sermon, *Sinners in the Hands of an Angry God* for the first time.

1742   Pennsylvania entrepreneur and Indian agent **George Croghan** establishes fur trade on the Ohio frontier.

1743   Scientist and inventor **Benjamin Franklin** begins his revolutionary experiments with electricity.

1743   Quaker minister **John Woolman** starts the first organized abolitionist movement.

1744   Carolina plantation manager **Eliza Lucas Pinckney** perfects the cultivation of indigo, a type of dye.

1748   German minister **Henry Melchior Mühlenberg** unites Lutheran churches in America.

1756   Eleven-year-old African prince **Olaudah Equiano** is kidnapped and sold into slavery.

1757   Botanist **Jane Colden** compiles a catalogue of native plants in the New York region.

1759   Mohegan preacher **Samson Occom** is ordained as a Christian minister.

1763   Failed rebellion staged by Ottawa war chief **Pontiac** marks the beginning of the end of the Native American way of life.

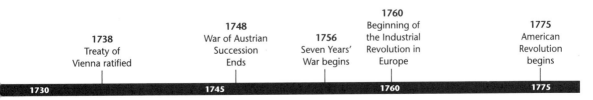

1760
Beginning of
the Industrial
Revolution in
Europe

1738
Treaty of
Vienna ratified

1748
War of Austrian
Succession
Ends

1756
Seven Years'
War begins

1775
American
Revolution
begins

1730   1745   1760   1775

Words to Know

A

Abolitionist: A person who takes measures to end slavery.

Absolute authority: Governing free from restraint.

American Revolution: 1775-83; a conflict in which American colonists gained independence from British rule.

Anarchist: One who rebels against any authority.

Antimonianism: The belief that faith alone is sufficient for salvation from sin. The view was considered heresy because it was contrary to the Puritan teaching that salvation can be gained only by doing good works.

B

Baptism: Initiation into the church in a ceremony that involves emersion in water or the sprinkling of water on the head.

Botanist: A specialist in plant life.

C

Calvinists: A religious group that places strong emphasis on the supreme power of God, the sinfulness of mankind, and the doctrine of predestination, which states that all human events are controlled by God.

Cannibalism: The eating of human flesh by another human being.

Capital offenses: Crimes that require a penalty of death.

Catechism: A summary or religious doctrine often in the form of questions and answers.

Charter: Title of land; a grant or guarantee from a sovereign power of a state or country.

Cholera: A disease marked by severe stomach problems.

The Church of England: The official religion of England; also known as the Anglican Church.

Classical school: A school devoted to the study of ancient languages and history.

Conquistador: Spanish military leader.

D

Decimated: Reduced drastically in number.

Dissenters: Those who question authority.

Dogma: Established opinion.

Dowry: The money or land brought by a bride to her husband at marriage.

E

Elegies: Pensive or reflective poems that are usually nostalgic or melancholy.

Emigrated: Moved from another country.

Excommunicated: Excluded from partaking in the rights of the church.

Exonerated: Cleared from accusation or blame.

F

Famine: An extreme scarcity of food.

Freeman: Former indentured servants who had gained their freedom; one who has the full rights of a citizen.

Friars: Members of a religious order who combine life as a monk with outside religious activity.

G

Great Awakening: A series of religious revivals that swept the American colonies near the middle of the eighteenth century.

H

Heretic: One who violates the laws of the church; one who does not conform to an accepted belief or doctrine.

Hybridization: The interbreeding of offspring of two animals or plants of different species.

Hydrography: The science of charting bodies of water.

I

Imported: To bring in from a foreign source.

Indentured servant: A person bound by signed documents to work as a laborer or household help for a specified time.

Insurrection: An act of revolt against civil authority or an established government.

L

Libel: Making a false statement that exposes another person to public dishonor.

M

Midwife: A person who assists women during childbirth.

Militia: Citizen's army.

Moravian Church: Sometimes known as United Brethren, it is a religion based on the forgiveness of sins through personal faith, strict interpretation of the Bible, and the importance of preaching the word of Jesus Christ instead of relying on church rituals.

Mutiny: A staged revolt or rebellion.

N

New World: A European term for North and South America.

Northwest Passage: The water route between the Atlantic and Pacific Oceans that the major world powers had long been seeking.

O

Ordained: Officially appointed with ministerial or priestly authority by the church.

Overseer: One who supervises workers.

P

Parliament: The supreme legislature body of government.

Patent: An official document giving a right to a piece of land.

Patron: One who gives financial support.

Pauper: One who cannot pay debts.

Pirate: A person who robs ships or plunders the land from the sea.

Plunderer: A person who steals by force.

Portage: To carry boats overland.

Privateer: A sailor on a privately owned ship who is authorized by a government to attack and capture enemy vessels.

Puritans: A religious group that believed in strict moral and spiritual codes.

Q

Quakers: Members of the Religious Society of Friends, which believes that the individual can receive divine truth from the Holy Spirit through his or her own "inner light" without the guidance of a minister or priest.

R

Roman Catholic Church: A Christian faith based in Rome, Italy, and headed by a pope who is considered unable of making a mistake and who oversees bishops, priests, and other clergy.

Royalists: Supporters of the king and queen.

S

Scripture: Passages from the Bible.

Scurvy: A disease caused by lack of vitamin C in the diet.

Sedition: Resistance against lawful authority.

Self-purification: Freeing oneself as an individual from sin.

Slave: A worker owned by and forced to work for someone else.

Smallpox: A highly contagious, often fatal, skin disease.

Speciman: An individual item typical of a whole.

Synod: An advisory council.

T

Tenent: A principle or doctrine.

Tenure: Term of holding a position or office.

Theologian: A specialist in the study of religion.

Topography: Configuration of a surface including the position of its natural and man-made features.

Tyrant: A ruler who brutally exercises absolute power.

V

Viceroy: One who rules in the name of the king.

W

Wampum: Beads used by Native Americans as money, ceremonial pledges, and ornaments.

Massasoit

c. 1580
Pokanoket, near present-day Bristol, Rhode Island
1661
Rhode Island

Wampanoag tribal leader

Massasoit was a Native American leader who worked to maintain friendly relations with English settlers in the early seventeenth century. He is also believed to have taken part in what has become known as the first Thanksgiving. While it is true that Massasoit strove for good relations with the Europeans, his story is more complicated than schoolbooks have led generations of Americans to believe. Massasoit maintained his treaty with the settlers even after a majority of Native Americans began to resist the colonists' expansion. As a result, he was criticized by other Native Americans for giving up too much in return for personal power and prestige.

Rules Wampanoags

From his home village of Pokanoket, near present-day Bristol, Rhode Island, Massasoit ruled the Wampanoags and a number of related tribes in southeastern New England. Little is known about Massasoit except that he was physically strong and, when conversing with the settlers, was "grave of countenance and spare of speech"—in other words, he was serious-looking and chose his words carefully. Dressed in traditional

" . . . not only the greatest King amongst them called Massasoit, but also all the Princes and people round about us, have either made suit unto us, or been glad of any occasion to make peace with us. . . . "

Plymouth Colony governor William Bradford.

Portrait: Massasoit.
Reproduced by permission of The Library of Congress.

Squanto

In 1614 an English sea captain kidnapped a number of Patuxent tribesmen who lived in the area where the Plymouth (Massachusetts) colonists landed. He sold them as slaves in Spain. Through a strange turn of events, one of the Patuxent men, Squanto was brought out of slavery by monks who wanted to convert him to Christianity. He later made his way to England and from there returned to his homeland. When he arrived, however, he was horrified to find his village abandoned. Tribeless, he joined Massasoit's people, the Wampanoags. When the Pilgrims arrived, Squanto followed Samoset, another Native American leader, out of the forest to greet them—in English—and helped them survive the harsh conditions in Plymouth. Squanto's friendship helped the colonists established a friendship with the far more powerful Massasoit.

Native American attire, with his face painted red and wearing a thick necklace of white beads (the sign of authority), Massasoit was a formidable (cause of fear or dread) presence. Although he initially frightened English settlers, he gave much-needed assistance and goodwill.

Pilgrims have hard winter

In 1620 about one hundred Pilgrims (early English settlers who wished to freely practice their own form of Christianity) arrived at Plymouth, Massachusetts. When their ship, the *Mayflower,* sailed back to England in the winter of 1620, it left behind a group of men, women, and children unprepared to deal with life in the wild land. As they shivered in their brush huts against the New England cold, they were surrounded by a "howling wilderness," an endless forest they imagined to be full of bloodthirsty savages, wolves, and maybe even devils. The new settlers did not know how to hunt, fish, plant, or build adequate shelters. They had few supplies to carry them through to spring. Under such terrible conditions, they struggled to stay alive. One by one the settlers died of malnutrition, disease, and gnawing hunger. Only half of them survived the first winter of 1620–21, and those who remained were weakened and confused, with little hope for the future. It seemed they would soon all be gone, dying thousands of miles from home on this wild, foreign shore, their bones dragged into the forest by fierce animals.

Massasoit comes to their rescue

Massasoit first appeared in the Plymouth Colony in March 1621. He followed Samoset, another Native American

leader, and **Squanto** (see entry), English-speaking Native Americans who paved the way for friendly relations with the English. When Massasoit and his sixty warriors stepped out of the wilderness and stood on a hilltop looking down on the settlement, the few surviving able-bodied colonists scrambled for their guns. But the settlers slowly realized they were not confronting enemies who wanted to kill them. Instead, the Native Americans turned out to be friendly people who gave them food in exchange for baubles (trinkets) and, moreover, helped protect them against marauding (roaming and raiding) Native American tribes. Massasoit seemed to be a blessing from Heaven. Squanto led the Native Americans in teaching the Pilgrims how to plant crops. After a bountiful harvest in the fall, the colonists had a feast of celebration to which they invited Massasoit and ninety of his men. Squanto was reportedly among them. This feast has come to be known as the first Thanksgiving, and Squanto in particular is associated with the event when it is commemorated each year in the United States.

Native American chief Massasoit arrives to negotiate peace with the Pilgrims. *Reproduced by permission of Corbis-Bettmann.*

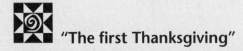

"The first Thanksgiving"

When the Pilgrims arrived at Plymouth, Massachusetts in 1620, they were not prepared to face a harsh winter in a strange environment. By spring 1621 many had died. Native American chief Massasoit and other Wampanoags came to the colonists' rescue, and an English-speaking Native American called Squanto taught them how to plant crops. After a bountiful harvest in the fall, the Pilgrims held a feast of celebration, to which they invited Massasoit and ninety of his men. In a letter dated 1621 and excerpted below, Plymouth governor **William Bradford** (see entry) described this event, which is now known as the first Thanksgiving.

A Letter Sent from New-England to a friend in these parts . . . .

. . . . We set the last Spring some twentie Acres of Indian-Corne, and sowed some six Acres of Barley and Peas, and according to the manner of the Indian, we manured our ground with Herrings or rather Shads [a type of fish], which we have in great abundance, and take with great ease at our doors. . . . Our harvest being gotten in, our Governor [Bradford is referring to himself] sent four men on fowling [hunting for birds], that so we might after a more special manner rejoice together, after we had gathered the fruit of our labors. They four in one day killed as much fowl, as with a little help beside, served the Company almost a week, at which time amongst other Recreations, we exercised our Arms [fired their weapons], many of the Indians coming amongst us, and amongst the rest their greatest King Massasoit, with some ninety men, whom for three days we entertained and feasted, and they went out and killed five Deer, which they brought to the Plantation [settlement] and bestowed on our Governor and upon the Captain, and others. And although it be not always so plentiful, as it was at this time with us, yet by the goodness of God, we are so far from want, that we often wish you partakers of our planty [plenty]. We have found the Indians very faithful in their Covenant of Peace with us; very loving and ready to pleasure us. We often go to them, and they come to us; some of us have been fifty miles by Land in the Country with them; the occasions and Relations whereof you shall understand by our general and more full Declaration of such things as are worth the noting. Yea it hath pleased God so to possess the Indians with a fear of us, and love unto us, that not only the greatest King amongst them called Massasoit, but also all the Princes and people round about us, have either made suit unto us [appealed to us], or been glad of any occasion to make peace with us. . . .

Reprinted in: Kupperman, Karen Ordahl, ed. Major Problems in American Colonial History. *Lexington, Mass.: D. C. Heath and Company, pp. 119–20.*

Massasoit and the Pilgrims also signed a peace treaty, which promised that the Native Americans and the English would live in harmony and that they would defend each other from outside attacks. Massasoit honored the treaty for the next forty years. During this time, the two groups exchanged numerous friendly visits. When Massasoit became ill, for instance, Plymouth colonists went to Pokanoket to treat their ally (one who is associated with another as a helper). On several occasions, Massasoit or his fellow Wampanoags probably saved the colonists from slaughter by warning them of possible attacks by warring tribes.

Massasoit in a difficult situation

Massasoit would later be criticized by other Native Americans for being too friendly with English settlers. At the time, however, he was in a difficult situation. Disease had recently ravaged his people. For this reason the number of Wampanoag warriors had greatly decreased, and their enemies wanted to take advantage of this fact. To the west, across Rhode Island at Narragansett Bay, roved the powerful Narragansett tribe, eager to slaughter Massasoit and the Wampanoags. To the east, the English, whatever their troubles, were rumored to have valuable trade goods and strange, new, "fire-breathing weapons" (guns). Caught between his traditional enemies to the west and the English on the coast to the east, Massasoit may have had little choice other than to ally himself with the newcomers. After all, they might be able to help the Wampanoags defend themselves.

All relations between Europeans and Native Americans had not been so congenial (pleasant), however. European contact with Native American tribes in the New England area had been happening for decades before the colonists established the Plymouth Colony, and there were many conflicts. Kidnappings and other incidents took place when European sea captains and fishermen threatened Native American territory. The Europeans also carried diseases, among them smallpox (a disease causing skin sores), typhus (a disease transmitted by body lice that causes high fever and other symptoms), and measles (a disease that causes a red skin rash). Lacking immunity from these diseases, whole Native American villages were devastated. Understandably, most of the Native Americans—even those who had not yet seen white men—thought of Europeans as bearers of deadly illnesses. Considering this, Massasoit's friendship was the exception to the general rule.

Copes with European invasion

Despite earnest efforts at goodwill, such as Massasoit's, the situation between the Wampanoags and their enemies was bound to get worse. New colonists starting other settlements cared nothing about honoring old agreements, such as the peace treaty between Massasoit and the Plymouth colonists. Having lived with little or no land of their own in Europe, these new colonists had not pulled up stakes and risked the dangerous, months-long voyage to be restrained upon their arrival. What they wanted was land of their own, and the land in the New World seemed theirs for the taking. All that stood in their way were the Native peoples, who fought back against the increasing invasion of the European settlers. Despite resistance from Native Americans, however, Europeans continued to expand into their territory.

In spite of these developments, Massasoit kept pressing for good relations with the Europeans. In his negotiations, he often valued the rights of the settlers over those of his own people. As a result, he weakened the Wampanoags in return for trade goods, personal fame, and security against his enemy, the Narragansetts. Critics claimed that while these things may have seemed necessary to Massasoit, they were hardly worth the price he paid for them.

Comes to resent colonists

Massasoit took an unpopular position by linking his fortunes to the English. As pressures against the Native Americans mounted, many of them decided to unite and either drive out the invaders or die in the attempt. Toward the end of his life, Massasoit, too, began to deeply resent the encroachment of the English settlers. Fourteen years after Massasoit's death, his son **Metacom** (also known as King Philip; see entry), initiated Metacom's War (also called King Philip's War; 1675–76) to win back the land his father had given away. Eventually involving several tribes and all the New England colonies, Metacom's War was the bloodiest conflict between Native Americans and colonists in the history of New England.

For further research

Biographical Dictionary of Indians of the Americas, Volume I. Newport Beach, Calif.: American Indian Publishers, 1991.

Bourne, Russell. *The Red King's Rebellion: Racial Politics in New England, 1675–1678.* New York: Atheneum, 1990.

Calloway, Colin G., ed. *After King Philip's War: Presence and Persistence in Indian New England.* Hanover, N.H.: Dartmouth College, 1978.

Kupperman, Karen Ordahl, ed. *Major Problems in American Colonial History.* Lexington, Mass.: D. C. Heath and Company, pp. 119–20.

Cotton Mather

March 19, 1663
Boston, Massachusetts
February 13, 1728
Boston, Massachusetts

Clergyman and scientist

"There is not a Fly but would confute [refute conclusively] an Atheist."

Cotton Mather.

Portrait: Cotton Mather.
Reproduced by permission of The Library of Congress.

Cotton Mather's life and work illustrate two sides of early American scientific thinking. As a Congregational (Puritan) clergyman and a firm believer in divine revelation (the word of God) and miracles, Mather accepted such unscientific notions as witchcraft. He supported the Salem witch trials, although he later changed his position. The author of hundreds of books and sermons, he ranks highly among the early American theologians. Yet he was also a leading scientist and only one of two colonial Americans to be elected to the Royal Society of London, a prestigious scientific organization in England. (**Benjamin Franklin** was the other American member; see entry.) Reconciling his interest in science with his religious views, Mather advocated the study of science as a means of teaching about God. A well-informed amateur physician (one who has no formal medical training), Mather was at the forefront of promoting medical advances such as the smallpox inoculation. (Smallpox is a highly contagious, often fatal, disease, and inoculation is the introduction of the disease-causing agent into the body in order to create resistance.) His book *The Angel of Bethesda,* a catalog of common ailments and their

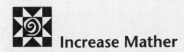

Increase Mather

Increase Mather, the father of Cotton Mather, was an historian and prominent Boston clergyman. He was also a leader in the scientific community. Increase Mather adopted the new ideas of such European scientists as Francis Bacon and Robert Hooke. He even incorporated scientific theories into his sermons. For instance, he tried to combat superstition by giving realistic explanations about comets and the nature of the universe. Newton's Comet of 1680 in particular inspired his interest in astronomy. Mather organized the Philosophical Club of Boston in 1683; one of the members was twenty-year-old Cotton Mather.

In 1684 Increase Mather wrote *Remarkable Providence,* and eight years later he actively supported the witch trials that began in Salem, Massachusetts. By 1693, however, he had changed his mind, calling the witch hunts a mistake in his book *Cases of Conscience Concerning Evil Spirits.* This work is credited with bringing the executions to an end. Mather served as president of Harvard College from 1685 until 1701.

remedies, made significant contributions to colonial American medicine. In spite of his success, however, Mather's personal life was filled with disappointment and anguish.

Must fulfill family expectations

Cotton Mather was born in Boston, Massachusetts, in 1663. At that time, Boston was the capital of American science. His father, Increase Mather, was an historian and prominent Boston clergyman. Cotton's grandfather was Richard Mather, a famous Puritan minister. (Puritanism is a branch of Christianity that stresses strict moral and spiritual codes.) His mother, Maria Cotton Mather, was the daughter of an equally esteemed Puritan minister, **John Cotton** (see entry). Such an impressive family background placed considerable pressure on Mather as a young boy. He was expected to become a successful theologian (a specialist in the study of religion) like his father and grandfathers, and he set about fulfilling these high expectations. By the time he was a teenager he had mastered

Cotton Mather witnesses witchcraft trials

Cotton Mather approved of the witchcraft trials held at Salem, Massachusetts, in 1692–93, during which nineteen people were executed. He published *Wonders of the Invisible World* (1693), defending the trials as being necessary in order to rid the colony of the influence of the Devil. An excerpt from the "The Trial of Martha Carrier," a chapter in Mather's book, describes a typical case that came before the Salem court.

At the Court of Oyer and Terminer [to hear and determine], Held by Adjournment at Salem, August 2, 1692

I. Martha Carrier was indicted [brought to trial] for the bewitching of certain persons, according to the form usual in such cases, pleading not guilty, to her indictment; there were first brought in a considerable number of the bewitched persons; who not only made the court sensible [aware] of an horrid witchcraft committed upon them, but also deposed [reported] that it was Martha Carrier, or her shape, that grievously tormented them by biting, pricking, pinching and choking of them. It was further deposed that while this Carrier was on her examination before the magistrates [judges], the poor people were so tortured that every one expected their death upon the very spot, but that upon the binding of Carrier they were eased. Moreover the look of Carrier then laid the afflicted people for dead; and her touch, if her eye at the same time were off them, raised them again: which things

Latin, Greek, and other ancient languages. He had also learned how to deliver formal religious sermons. When Mather was fifteen he graduated from Harvard College in Boston, and three years later he earned a master's degree. In 1685, when he was twenty-two, he was ordained (officially appointed by the church) as his father's colleague in the ministry at the prestigious Second Church in Boston. The following year Mather married Abigail Phillips.

Caught between religion and science

Soon Mather was a prominent member of New England's powerful and influential class. At the same time he found himself involved in a period of profound religious and social change. Although he and his father were preaching the strict Puritanism introduced by the founding fathers of the Massachusetts colony, Mather realized his world was changing. New scientific ideas were rapidly reaching the American

were also now seen upon her trial. And it was testified that upon the mention of some having their necks twisted almost round, by the shape of this Carrier, she replied, "It's no matter though their necks had been twisted quite off."

II. Before the trial of this prisoner, several of her own children had frankly and fully confessed not only that they were witches themselves, but that this their mother had made them so. This confession they made with great shows of repentance, and with much demonstration of truth. They related place, time, occasion; they gave an account of journeys, meetings and mischiefs by them performed, and were very credible in what they said. Nevertheless, this evidence was not produced against the prisoner at the bar [in court], inasmuch as there was other evidence enough to proceed upon. . . . After recording the testimony of numerous witnesses, Mather attached this note: Memorandum. This rampant hag, Martha Carrier, was the person of whom the confessions of the witches, and of her own children among the rest, agreed that the Devil had promised her she should be Queen of Heb [Queen of Hebrews].

Mather later reversed his position and supported the view that the witch hunts had been unjustified.

Reprinted in: Elliot, Emory, and others, eds. American Literature: a Prentice Hall Anthology. Englewood Cliffs, N.J.: Prentice Hall, 1991, p. 190.

colonies from Europe, and many of these theories undermined the traditional teachings of Christianity. For instance, Christians believed that God created and controlled the universe, whereas scientists were arguing that man could learn about the world by observing and studying nature itself. In fact, from a scientific perspective, a divine creator seemed to have no place in scientific analysis.

Throughout his life Mather continued to preach traditional Christian principles. In the spirit of the Puritan fathers, he warned his congregations that God would punish unrepentant (not regretful) sinners. Mather claimed that God spoke to him in thunderstorms and appeared to him in the form of angels. Like his father, Mather approved of the witchcraft trials and executions held at Salem, Massachusetts, in the winter 1692–93. These trials were the result of some teenage girls in Salem who identified several people as witches (those who can control events through the use of supernatural powers). By the time the hysteria finally died down, 156 suspected witches were in prison (most of them women), and 19 people were eventually executed. Mather published *Wonders of the Invisible World* (1693), in which he defended the trials as being necessary to rid the colony of the influence of the Devil. Mather later reversed his position and—again like his father—supported the view that the witch hunts had been unjustified and excessive.

Pursues science with religion

Despite his success as a minister, Mather felt a strong pull toward science. Consequently, for forty years he struggled to make a connection between two apparently opposite world views. He firmly believed in the literal truth of the Bible (the holy book of the Christian faith), and he never doubted that God controlled world affairs. Nevertheless, when he was in his thirties he became one of the leading scientists of the early eighteenth century. In an effort to reconcile religion with science, he asserted that the world was created by God and but could be understood through scientific study. Mather's first publication was an analysis of the validity of the story of Noah's Ark. (According to the Old Testament, the first part of the Bible, Noah was a Jewish patriarch, or one of the original leaders of the Jews. He built a boat in which he, his family, and living creatures of every kind survived a flood that destroyed the rest of the world.)

In 1690 Mather wrote: "There is not a Fly but would confute an *Atheist*." In other words, even the tiniest creature in nature will disprove the argument of a person who claims that there is no God. His masterpiece, *Magnalia Christi Americana* (a religious history of New England), appeared in 1702. Admitted to the Royal Society in 1713, he studied the work of such European scientists as Robert Boyle and Isaac Newton. Mather published his views about the connection between religion and science in *The Christian Philosopher* (1721). In this work he argued that everything in the universe has a reason and a purpose. According to Mather, the natural world glorifies the wisdom of God, who with perfect efficiency made only necessary things. By the end of his life Mather had published more than four hundred books and sermons. Numerous other works remained in manuscript (unpublished) form upon his death.

Encourages smallpox inoculation

During this time Mather pursued other wide-ranging scientific interests. He wrote about fossils, astronomy, mathematics, zoology, entomology (a branch of zoology that deals with insects), ornithology (a branch of zoology dealing with birds), and botany (the study of plants). Like other clergymen, he studied and practiced medicine as an amateur. In his autobiography he explained that his attraction to medicine resulted from his own hypochondria (having imagined illnesses). When he was a teenager he had an intense curiosity about medical literature. Devouring book after book, he eventually imagined that he himself had the symptoms of the diseases he was reading about. Over the years Mather became an authority on the causes and cures of mental illness, measles, scurvy (a disease caused by lack of vitamin C), fevers, and smallpox. In fact, in 1721 he was the foremost advocate of smallpox inoculation in America. Mather possibly promoted this new technique because two of his fifteen children and one of his three wives had died from smallpox.

Writes medical manual

In 1722 Mather wrote *The Angel of Bethesda,* a detailed study of the prevention and cure of common illnesses. Arguing that disease is the result of sin, he found a direct connection between the mind and the body. He also discussed techniques of psychotherapy (treatment of mental illness). Another important feature of the work was Mather's explanation of microorganisms (germs) as the cause of disease, a theory then being debated in Europe but not yet well known in America. Mather also kept a diary (published in 1911, 1912, and 1976), which ultimately reached seventeen volumes. The diary reveals the extent of Mather's anguish and profound disappointment in life.

Experiences setbacks and tragedy

Despite his achievements, Mather was constantly experiencing personal setbacks and tragedy. After the death of his first wife, Abigail, with whom he had a happy marriage, he wed Elizabeth Clark Hubbard in 1703. He and Elizabeth were happy together, but she too died at a young age. Mather's third marriage, to Lydia Lee George, was disastrous: Lydia reportedly ruined him financially before she went insane. With his three wives Mather had fifteen children, but only two were living at the time of his death in 1728. Only a few months before he died he completed *Paterna,* a book he wrote for his children, in which he portrayed his own death as being exactly like Christ's crucifixion. (Jesus of Nazareth, also called Christ, was the founder of Christianity. He was put to death by being nailed to a cross, or crucified.) Neither of Mather's children, however, was capable of carrying on the intellectual tradition of three previous generations of Mathers. For instance, Mather's son Increase—named for Mather's father—preferred to spend his time in pubs instead of preparing for the ministry. Yet Cotton Mather was even more disappointed in himself than he was in his children. When he was not chosen to succeed his father as president of Harvard College, he concluded that he was a failure because he had not carried on the Mather tradition.

For further research

Elliot, Emory, and others, eds. *American Literature: a Prentice Hall Anthology.* Englewood Cliffs, N.J.: Prentice Hall, 1991, p. 190.

Levin, David. *Cotton Mather: The Young Life of the Lord's Remembrancer, 1663–1703.* Cambridge, Mass.: Harvard University Press, 1978.

The Puritans: American Literature Colonial Period (1608-1700). http://www.falcon.jmu.edu/-ramseyil/amicol.htm Available July 13, 1999.

Silverman, Kenneth. *The Life and Times of Cotton Mather.* New York: Harper & Row, 1984.

Wendell, Barrett. *Cotton Mather.* New York: Chelsea House, 1980.

Metacom (King Philip)

c. 1640
Southeastern Massachusetts
August 12, 1676
Mount Hope

Native American leader

Metacom (also known as King Philip) was the chief of the Wampanoag tribe. He headed the Native American resistance to colonial power in southern New England during the seventeenth century. Colonists celebrated his death, an event that marked their victory in the conflict named for him, King Philip's War (1675–76), and assured English dominance in the region. Critics of the Puritans (people who believe in a branch of Christianity that stressed strict moral and religious codes), however, portrayed Metacom as a hero and condemned those who pushed him to war. These differing opinions reflect the changing alliances and power structures that existed before King Philip's War.

Remains wary of colonists

Metacom was born around 1640 in present-day southeastern Massachusetts. As he was growing up he was sensitive to the increasing population of English newcomers. He was one of five children of **Massasoit** (see entry), a Wampanoag chieftain who had aided and cooperated with Pilgrim colonists in Plymouth. Massasoit has been criticized for selling too

Portrait: Metacom (King Philip). *Reproduced by permission of Archive Photos, Inc.*

much Native American land to the English in exchange for their support. After Massasoit died in 1660, his eldest son, Wamsutta, told Plymouth settlers that he was now *sachem* (chief) of the Wampanoags. When Wamsutta asked for English names for himself and his brother Metacom, he was given the name Alexander and Metacom was dubbed Philip. Plymouth colonists captured Wamsutta when he began selling land to other colonies. Metacom suspected that his brother had been poisoned when he died in 1662. When Metacom himself became *sachem,* he remained wary of the Plymouth colonists.

Involved in land disputes

From 1662 to 1675, Metacom worked to maintain his power as chief and to ensure his people's welfare. Meanwhile, the English population—and English power—continued to grow. At the same time, the Wampanoag Confederacy, which consisted of many villages and families, apparently began to splinter. This was due in part to the influence of colonial authorities and missionaries. Metacom's territory formed a border zone between Plymouth Colony, Rhode Island, and the Massachusetts Bay Colony capital in Boston, each of which wanted the area. In order to hold onto his political influence, the *sachem* sold tracts of land in the region to various colonists. Resulting conflicts over the borders of these lands, however, were rarely settled to his satisfaction. Colonial courts seemed biased and insensitive to the concerns of Native Americans. The tribes were also angered by colonial efforts to influence their politics.

The conflict regarding landownership reached a crisis in 1667. In violation of an agreement with Metacom, the Plymouth Colony authorized the purchase of land within his territory for the town of Swansea. Tribal war parties, possibly led by Metacom, began to appear near Swansea in an effort to intimidate the colonists. In 1671 Plymouth demanded a meeting with the chief. When he arrived, the colony's leaders compelled him at gunpoint to surrender his people's firearms and to sign a treaty. This treaty placed Metacom—and even his dead brother and father—under Plymouth's authority and thus challenged previous land sales to other colonies. Metacom complained to Massachusetts Bay Colony authorities, but he received no assistance. Instead, both Plymouth and Massa-

Narragansetts: enemies of the Wampanoags

The Narragansetts were an Algonquian-speaking people who lived in the region that is now Rhode Island. During the seventeenth century they were the strongest Native American tribe in southern New England, and a major enemy of the Wampanoags. When the Narragansetts managed to survive the European plague that swept the area in 1617, they were joined by many smaller tribes. Although the Wampanoags were also struck by the plague, their chief, **Massasoit** (see entry), became allied to the English. In 1636 the Narragansetts sold land to **Roger Williams** (see entry), a founder of Rhode Island, who convinced them to join the Massachusetts colonists in the Pequot War (1637).

Although the Narragansetts were originally enemies of the Wampanoags and allies of the English, the situation changed dramatically in 1675. Late that year colonists

began attacking Narragansett villages in the Connecticut River valley. In retaliation, the Narragansetts became allies of the Wampanoags during King Philip's War (1675–76) in effort to drive out white settlers. In response, the colonists then joined forces with the powerful Mohawks, and quickly defeated the Wampanoag-Narragansett alliance. This conflict, which ended with the murder of Wampanoag chief Metacom, led to English dominance in southeastern New England. Ironically, the Narragansetts suffered the same fate as their former enemy, as many Native American tribes were destroyed as a result of the war. The Narragansetts lost a thousand men in a battle known as the Great Swamp Fight. Survivors either migrated or joined other tribes. Although they had numbered five thousand in 1674, by 1832 there were only eighty surviving members of the once-great Narragansett tribe.

chusetts Bay forced him to sign a new treaty that gave the Wampanoags no land rights.

Wants support for uprising

At about this time Metacom evidently began planning the uprising that came to be known as King Philip's War. Although he received the backing of other Wampanoag leaders, Metacom knew that the tribe was too small to fight the English alone. Therefore, he sought support from other tribes. He managed to gain the support of groups such as the Nipmucks, who also felt threatened by the colonists. He had difficulty, however, in establishing an alliance with the Narragansetts, who were major enemies of the Wampanoags. The rivalry between the two tribes dated back many years. In fact, it was this conflict that had compelled Metacom's father, Massasoit, to sell Native American land to the English for protection against the Narragansetts. Metacom was now seeking the support of the Narragansetts only because they were the most powerful tribe in the region.

The events leading up to King Philip's War put Metacom in a difficult position. At the time, he still had not gained enough support to launch an uprising. He was thereby forced to play a waiting game, whereby he tried to prevent his angry warriors from raiding colonial villages and still keep them loyal to him. Rumors of Metacom's efforts soon reached colonial authorities. About this time, the body of John Sassamon, a Native American, was found in a pond. It turned out that Sassamon had told the English about Metacom's plan. The colonists tried three Wampanoags for the murder; they were subsequently found guilty and hanged. The English based their case entirely on the testimony of another Native American. On the scaffold (platform where criminals are hanged or beheaded) one of the three supposedly confessed Metacom's guilt in the murder of Sassamon.

King Philip's War begins and ends

In July 1675 Metacom's men, angered by the recent events, launched the conflict that became known as King Philip's War. The uprising was apparently touched off more by the rage of Metacom's people than by any master plan. When a colonial army tried to capture the *sachem* near his home on Mount Hope (present-day Bristol, Rhode Island), he escaped with his warriors and their families. Then, joining forces with his Nipmuck allies, Metacom attacked and burned villages west and south of Boston. Native American groups in the Connecticut River valley also rose in revolt when anxious colonists overreacted to the violence. Finally, in late December, the Narragansetts joined the uprising after English forces attacked their village. During the ensuing winter, joint Native American raiding parties burned several colonial towns, sending refugees streaming into Boston. Although Metacom did not actually command this informal army—in December he had gone to the

General Goffe battling the Native Americans at Hadley during King Philip's War. *Reproduced by permission of Archive Photos, Inc.*

Hudson River valley to seek the support of other Native groups—his power seemed to extend throughout the entire region.

Metacom's flaming star was soon extinguished, however. While on his quest for new alliances, the Mohawk tribe and their New York colonial allies attacked his band, killing all but forty of his men and destroying the *sachem's* prestige. The Mohawks continued their attacks from the west, while colonial forces, joined by other Native American allies, became more effective. These groups, who were not Wampanoag allies, eventually brought about Metacom's downfall. Disease and hunger also took a terrible toll. By the spring of 1676 the informal Native alliance broke apart. Many bands moved north or west out of harm's way, and some made peace with the colonists. Metacom headed for home after his allies threatened to send his head to the English as a peace offering.

As the uprising dissolved, some of the *sachem's* former

supporters formed a squad and hunted Metacom. The chief's wife and son were captured and apparently, like most captured Native Americans, sold in the West Indies as slaves. Finally, on August 12, 1676, Metacom and his dwindling band were surrounded. Metacom was shot by a Native American serving with the colonial forces. The *sachem's* head was cut off and hacked into quarters, then the pieces were sent to the colonial capitals. A Wampanoag legend, however, holds that Metacom's warriors stole his head and secretly buried it near Mount Hope, where his spirit still periodically speaks.

Causes of King Philip's War

King Philip's War demonstrates the changing alliances that had long existed in southern New England. Originally, the central conflict was between the Wampanoags, their enemy the Narragansetts, and the newly arrived English settlers. It was this conflict that had prompted Metacom's father, Massasoit, to maintain friendly relations with the English by selling them land. Some historians believe that Massasoit sold his tribe's birthright for protection against the Narragansetts. They also believe that King Philip's War was Metacom's attempt to win back the land his father had given away. The participation of the Narragansetts in the war represented a major shift in alliances and disrupted many long-standing relationships between Native American groups. Therefore, it comes as no surprise that Metacom was murdered by other Native Americans. The defeat of Metacom and his allies decimated (reduced drastically in number) the Native population. The colonists also suffered high casualties, but they eventually regained dominance in the region. While many Indian communities survived, Metacom's death marked the end of Native independence in southern New England.

For further research

Cwiklik, Robert. *King Philip and the War with the Colonists*. Englewood Cliffs, N.J.: Silver Burdett Publishers, 1989.

The Indian Wars. http://www.geocities.com/Heartland/Hills/1094/indian.htm Available July 13, 1999.

Sewall, Marcia. *Thunder from the Clear Sky*. Old Tappan, N.J.: Simon and Schuster Children's, 1995.

Webb, Stephen Saunders. *1676: The End of American Independence*. New York: Knopf, 1984.

Thomas Morton

1579?
England
1647
Maine

Massachusetts fur trader and author

Thomas Morton had a colorful career in the Massachusetts Bay Colony as a fur trader and critic of Puritanism (a branch of Christianity that stressed strict moral and spiritual codes). Soon after arriving in Massachusetts he set up a fur-trading post called Merry Mount, where he sold rum and guns to Native Americans. Much to the disapproval of Plymouth settlers, Merry Mount attracted rowdy colonists, Native Americans, and even pirates (people who rob ships or plunder the land from the sea). On May Day 1627, Morton infuriated the Puritans by building a giant Maypole and hosting a celebration with drinking, dancing, and merrymaking. Massachusetts authorities twice deported (forcibly sent out of the country) him to England before sending him to Maine. Morton is also remembered as the author of *New English Canaan* (1637), a history of New England that gives one of the few non-Puritan accounts of early colonial life in Massachusetts.

Establishes Merry Mount

Thomas Morton was born in England around 1579, but little is known about his early life. After receiving a good edu-

"The setting up of this Maypole was a lamentable spectacle to the precise separatists that lived at new Plymouth."

Thomas Morton.

Portrait: Thomas Morton.
Reproduced by permission of Archive Photos, Inc.

219

cation, he ran a successful law practice in the west of England. In 1621 he married a widow named Alice Miller. Reportedly a disreputable person, Morton is said to have mistreated his wife and was supposedly suspected of having committed murder. In 1622 Morton took a three-month trip to New England. Realizing the opportunity there, three years later he sailed on the ship *Unity* to the Massachusetts Bay Colony with a company headed by a Captain Wollaston. When they arrived in Massachusetts, Wollaston founded a settlement called Mount Wollaston (now the city of Quincy) and Morton set up a trading post, which he named Merry Mount. According to Morton's account in *New English Canaan,* Merry Mount was a translation of Pasonagessit, the Native American name for the site.

When Wollaston moved to Virginia, Morton took control of Mount Wollaston (some historians say he renamed the town Merry Mount). He immediately had problems with Massachusetts authorities—particularly the Plymouth settlers (Puritan Separatists who called themselves Pilgrims), who were led by Governor **William Bradford** (see entry). The Puritans disapproved of Morton and his companions because they were Anglicans (members of the Church of England, which the Puritan Separatists had left to form their own religious group). Plymouth citizens also objected to Morton's trading post, where he sold whiskey, guns, and ammunition to Native Americans in exchange for furs. Moreover, in violation of the law, he showed the Native Americans how to use firearms. But the Puritans were especially annoyed because he had interfered with their own fur trading activities. For instance, in 1625 the Plymouth settlers opened their first trade route in Maine. Morton followed them and established contacts with Native Americans. When the Plymouth colonists set up a permanent trading post at Kennebec three years later, they found that for the past two seasons Morton had been taking the choicest furs.

Maypole angers Puritans

Plymouth authorities claimed that Merry Mount undermined morality in the Massachusetts Bay Colony. Bradford wrote in his history of Plymouth, *Of Plymouth Plantation* (first published in 1857), that Merry Mount was a "den of iniquity [sin]." Morton's establishment attracted drunken

carousers (people who drink liquor freely) and men of questionable character—historians say it was a favorite meeting place for pirates. Even worse, Christians came there to drink rum and often socialized with Native Americans. Morton's troubles reached a peak on May Day 1627 when he built his eighty-foot Maypole at Merry Mount and hosted a noisy celebration. (A Maypole is a tall flower-wreathed pole that was often the center of May Day sports and dances. May Day was a

The raising of the Maypole, in preparation for the Maypole dance.
Reproduced by permission of Corbis-Bettman.

From "The Maypole of Merry-Mount"

On May Day 1627 Thomas Morton erected his infamous Maypole at Merry Mount and hosted a noisy celebration. Colonists and Native Americans enjoyed a day of drinking, dancing, and frolicking. The Puritans, who were strictly religious, were upset by the celebration because they viewed May Day as a non-Christian ritual. Morton described the event in the following excerpt from his book *New English Canaan* (he referred to himself as "my host").

The Inhabitants of Pasonagessit (having translated the name of their habitation from that ancient savage name

to Merry-Mount) did devise amongst themselves to have it performed in a solemn manner with revels [a wild party] and merriment after the old English custom. They prepared to set up a Maypole . . . and brewed a barrel of excellent beer, and provided a case of bottles to be spent, with other good cheer, for all comers of that day. And because they would have it in a complete form, they had prepared a song fitting to the time and present occasion. And upon Mayday they brought the Maypole to the place appointed, with drums, guns, pistols, and other fitting instruments, for that purpose; and there erected it with the help of Savages, that came there to see the manner of our revels. A goodly pine tree, eighty feet long, was

celebration held in medieval England on May 1, in the tradition of the spring fertility rites of Egypt and India.) Colonists and Native Americans enjoyed a day of drinking and dancing. The Puritans were furious because they considered the event to be a pagan (non-Christian) ritual. Resolving to shut down Merry Mount, Plymouth officials tried unsuccessfully to reason with Morton over the next several months.

Sent back to England

In 1628 a company of men led by Miles Standish arrested Morton. He managed to escape but was soon recaptured and charged with selling guns to Native Americans. He was then deported to England for trial. After Morton's departure **John Endecott** (see entry), governor of the Massachusetts Company, took over the management of Merry Mount. Endecott had the Maypole chopped down, and he changed the name of the place to Mount Dagon. Morton was finally acquitted (found innocent) of the charges in England, so he returned

reared up, with a pair of buck's horns nailed on, somewhat near unto the top of it: where it stood as a fair sea mark for directions; how to find out the way to my host of Merry-Mount. . . .

The setting up of this Maypole was a lamentable spectacle to the precise separatists that lived at new Plymouth. They termed it an Idol [image of a pagan god] . . . and stood at defiance with the place, naming it Mount Dagon; threatening to make it a woeful mount not a merry mount. . . .

There was likewise a merry song made, which (to make their revels more fashionable) was sung with a chorus, every man bearing his part; which they performed in a dance, hand in hand about the Maypole while one of the Company sung, and filled out the good liquor. . . .

This harmless mirth [gaiety and laughter] made by young men (that lived in hope to have wives brought over to them . . .) was much distasted by the precise Separatists . . . troubling their brains more than reason would require about things that are indifferent, and from that time sought occasion against my honest host of Merry-Mount to overthrow his undertakings, and to destroy his plantation quite and clean.

Reprinted in: Colbert, David, ed. Eyewitness to America. New York: Pantheon Books, 1997, pp. 25–26.

to Massachusetts. He resumed trading with the Native Americans and stirred up opposition to Endecott among the colonists. In 1630 he was again arrested, more or less for being a public nuisance. Historians speculate that he may also have been a spy in the employ of Ferdinando Gorges, head of the Council of New England, who wanted to make New England a royal colony. (A royal colony was directly controlled by the English monarch.)

Before deporting Morton to England again, Massachusetts authorities placed him in stocks (a device used for public punishment), took all of his property, and burned down his house. Morton was acquitted a second time and remained in England for over a decade. During this time he worked as a legal counsel for Gorges, who was trying to revoke the charter (a contract issued by the English Crown that gave a group of settlers the right to start a colony and establish a government) of the Massachusetts Bay Company (see **John Winthrop** entry). In the mid-1630s Morton wrote *New English Canaan*, in which he encouraged others to seek their fortune in New England. ("Canaan" in the title refers to the Promised Land, or destined home, of the Israelites in the Christian Bible. Likewise, New England was the promised land of the Puritans, who sought religious and political freedom.) Yet he also ridiculed Puritan manners and narrow-mindedness, depicting the Native Americans as being more Christian than the Puritans themselves. Although the book upset the Puritans, Morton returned to Massachusetts in 1643. He was immediately arrested and jailed in Boston for two years. Upon his release in 1645, Massachusetts officials forced him to go to Maine, which was being colonized by Gorges.

Morton died in poverty in 1647. Although he was unknown at the time of his death, *New English Canaan* became a classic, satirical account of early colonial life and influenced several American writers. Among them was Nathaniel Hawthorne, an author who was harshly critical of the Puritans. In addition to such tales as *The Scarlet Letter,* Hawthorne wrote *The Maypole of Merrymount,* which was based on Morton's infamous May Day celebration.

For further research

Colbert, David, ed. *Eyewitness to America.* New York: Pantheon Books, 1997, pp. 25–26.

Connors, Donald Francis. *Thomas Morton.* New York: Twayne Publishers, 1969.

Elliott, Emory, and others, eds. *American Literature: A Prentice Hall Anthology.* Englewood Cliffs, N.J., 1991, pp. 105–06.

Johnson, Allen, and others, eds. *Dictionary of American Biography.* New York: Scribner, 1946–1958, p. 267.

Stephen, Leslie, and Sidney Lee, eds. *The Dictionary of National Biography.* London, England: Oxford University Press, 1917, pp. 1055–57.

Henry Melchior Mühlenberg

September 11, 1711
Hanover (a former state of Germany)
October 7, 1787
Trappe, Pennsylvania

Founder of the American Lutheran Church

Henry Melchior Mühlenberg is known as the "father of the American Lutheran Church." (The Lutheran Church is a Christian religious organization founded by Martin Luther in opposition to the Roman Catholic Church.) He is credited with almost single-handedly uniting the scattered and directionless Lutheran churches in the American colonies. He was later instrumental in organizing the Pennsylvania Ministerium, a central church organization that served the massive numbers of German immigrants (people who move from one country and settle in another) who arrived during the latter part of the eighteenth century.

Trains for ministry

Henry Melchior Mühlenberg was born on September 6, 1711, in Hanover (then a state in Germany). His father was a shoemaker who was active in the local Lutheran church. Mühlenberg attended a classical school (a school devoted to the study of ancient languages and history) and received extensive instruction in Latin. After his father died, a local minister taught him to play the organ, which inspired a life-

"Let the Church be Planted."

Henry Melchior Mühlenberg.

Portrait: Henry Melchior Mühlenberg. *Reproduced by permission of Corbis-Bettmann.*

long love of music. Well-connected family friends, recognizing his talents, sent him to the University of Göttingen and then to Halle, the great center for the study of religion. At Halle, Mühlenberg continued his studies in languages and music, helped found an orphanage (a home for children without parents), and worked as a teacher. He was ordained (officially appointed by the church) as a minister in the Lutheran Church in 1735. (The Lutheran Church was the first Protestant denomination; see box.) Mühlenberg's future was altered when his former instructors at Halle convinced him to go to America. At that time large numbers of German immigrants were moving to the American colonies. Three Lutheran congregations in Pennsylvania, which had neither church buildings nor pastors, had appealed to church officials in Halle for assistance. Mühlenberg was to be the solution to their problem.

Finds total chaos

In 1742 Mühlenberg sailed to Charleston, South Carolina, surviving one Atlantic storm after another. Upon finally reaching Charleston he visited the Salsburger Lutherans before going on to Philadelphia, Pennsylvania. In Philadelphia a different storm awaited him when he found that his congregation had been split. Some members were following a recently arrived minister, Nicholas Ludwig von Zinzendorf, a Lutheran who also advocated Moravian beliefs. (The Moravian Church, sometimes known as United Brethren or Herrnhuters, is based on forgiveness of sins through personal faith, strict interpretation of the Bible, and the importance of preaching the word of Christ instead of relying on church rituals.) Meanwhile several others had joined a congregation at Providence, which had actually been assigned to Mühlenberg. This group was being led by the Valentine Kraft, a minister who had emigrated from Germany. Mühlenberg's third congregation was headed by an alcoholic pastor known only as "Schmed."

Rather than confront Zinzendorf, Kraft, and Schmed directly, Mühlenberg relied on the fact that he had been sent to Pennsylvania by King George III of England (who also ruled Hanover). Mühlenberg met with followers of Kraft and Schmed, then he took control of their congregations. But Zinzendorf was a more difficult adversary because he had led a virtuous life. Mühlenberg persisted because Zinzendorf wanted

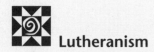

Lutheranism

Lutheranism was the first Protestant Christian denomination. The Lutheran Church was founded in 1520 by German theologian Martin Luther, who initiated the Protestant Reformation, a revolution within the Roman Catholic Church. (The Roman Catholic Church is a Christian faith based in Rome, Italy, and headed by a pope who is considered infallible and who oversees bishops, priests, and other clergy. The Catholic worship service is called a Mass, and priests are empowered to forgive Catholics of their sins.) Luther protested, among other things, the corruption and misuse of power among the Catholic clergy—priests, bishops, and popes—who had become wealthy through their association with the church. For instance, they required church members to pay money for forgiveness of sins. Disgusted by such greed and abuse of power, Luther advocated a radical departure from traditional Catholic practices and doctrine (church laws). According to Luther, the Scriptures (the Bible, the holy book of the Christian faith) are the only source of truth, and it is the right of the individual to interpret the Scriptures without the aid of priests. In addition, forgiveness of sins comes directly from God and not through the clergy. Almost from the beginning, the Lutherans themselves disagreed over interpretation of the Bible and the proper form of the worship service. Many wanted no association with Catholics or Calvinists (Protestants who believe in strict adherence to the Scriptures), while others wanted to associate with other Christian groups. Today there is no single religious philosophy governing the various branches of the Lutheran Church in Germany, Scandinavia, and North America. Nevertheless most place great emphasis on preaching and congregational singing

---

to unite Christians of all denominations under Moravianism, and Mühlenberg considered this a violation of the doctrines of the Lutheran Church. Eventually Zinzendorf had to back down because Mühlenberg had been officially licensed to lead the Philadelphia congregation.

Revitalizes American Lutheranism

Mühlenberg soon became a powerful religious leader. As he traveled throughout the American colonies he founded new churches and brought old congregations together. To get rid of fraudulent (deceitful) ministers, he kept up a steady correspondence with church officials at Halle. By focusing attention on the colonies, Mühlenberg attracted well-trained and devoted Lutheran ministers. His message was accessible to early settlers because he preached widely and constantly in German, English, Dutch, and even Latin—whatever language was required by circumstances. Mühlenberg also adapted the content and style of his sermons to the preferences of his audiences. He avoided public controversies that might drive away church members. He attracted converts and rallied congregations to erect or enlarge church buildings for regular worship. In 1745 he married the daughter of Conrad Weiser, the commissioner of Indian affairs for Pennsylvania. The Mühlenbergs eventually had eleven children, all of whom survived to occupy prominent positions.

Unites congregations

Throughout his career Mühlenberg abided by the motto: "Let the Church be Planted." His goal was realized in 1748 when six Swedish and German pastors met with twenty-four American church delegates (representatives) in Pennsylvania. They formed the Pennsylvania Ministerium, a central organization, and unified the Lutheran congregations. Mühlenberg was appointed head of the Ministerium. The pastors also compiled a book of common prayer (a text used in all worship services) that remained in use until the nineteenth century. Whenever conflicts arose, Mühlenberg successfully acted as peacemaker. In 1760 he joined Swedish church leader Karl Wrangel in reorganizing the Ministerium. Mühlenberg and Wrangel issued written constitutions and laid the foundation for continuing cooperation among the congregations throughout the country.

Mühlenberg remained a loyal subject of King George III until the signing of the Declaration of Independence. (Adopted July 4, 1776, the Declaration of Independence was a document that declared the independence of the thirteen American colonies from British rule and established them as the United States.) Mühlenberg died on October 7, 1787. That same year the Lutheran and German Reformed Churches joined forces to found Franklin College in Pennsylvania. Mühlenberg's son, Henry Ernest, was named the first president.

For further research

The Journals of Henry Melchior Mühlenberg. Translated by Theodore G. Tappart and John W. Doberstein. Rockport, Maine: Picton Press, 1993.

Riforgiato, Leonard R. *Missionary of Moderation: Henry Melchior Mühlenberg and the Lutheran Church in English America.* Lewisburg, Penn.: Bucknell University Press, 1980.

Wallace, Paul A. W. *The Mühlenbergs of Pennsylvania.* Philadelphia: University of Pennsylvania Press, 1950.

Samson Occom

1723
New London, Connecticut
1792
Stockbridge, New York

Mohegan preacher, diarist, and hymn lyricist

" . . . I began to think about the Christian Religion, and was under great trouble of Mind for Some Time."

Samson Occom.

Portrait: Samson Occum.
Reproduced by permission of Archive Photos, Inc.

Samson Occom was a significant figure in the religious life of eighteenth-century America. He began his career as a Mohegan (a Native American tribe) minister and missionary in the late colonial period, during a time when many Native Americans and colonists were converted to Christianity known as the Great Awakening. Later, Occom became the first Native American to publish a text—a sermon—in the English language. Through his writings—which also included diaries, letters, and hymn lyrics—he defended his Native American culture. As a preacher he solicited funds for Eleazer Wheelock's charity school, which was dedicated to the education and conversion of young Native Americans (see box). Money raised by Occom in England also led indirectly to Wheelock's establishment of Dartmouth College. In spite of his achievements, however, Occom and his family lived in poverty. Historians have confirmed Occom's claim that he was subjected to racist treatment by church authorities, who refused to pay him a salary equal to that of an English minister.

"I was Born a Heathen"

Occom reported being born in a wigwam in 1723 to Sarah, a descendant of the legendary Mohegan leader Uncas, and Joshua, "a great Hunter" and one of three sons of Tomock-ham (also called Ashneon). He wrote: "I was Born a Heathen in Mmoyouheeunnuck alias Mohegan in N[ew] London—North America. my [sic] Parents were altogether Heathens, and I was Educated by them in their Heathenish Notions. . . . [They] in particular Were very Strong in the Customs of their fore Fathers." When he reached age sixteen, he said, "there was a great Stir of Religion in these parts of the World both amongst the Indians as Well as the English, and about this Time I began to think about the Christian Religion, and was under great trouble of Mind for Some Time."

Becomes a Christian

By "great Stir of Religion" Occom meant the Great Awakening and its widespread impact on communities throughout the colonies (see **Jonathan Edwards** and **George Whitefield** entries). At that time he was one of twelve councillors to *sachem* (chief) Ben Uncas. However, Occom's mother Sarah, who was a Christian convert (one who leaves one religion to join another), wanted him also to adopt the European religion. In 1743 she convinced Eleazer Wheelock, a famous Calvinist minister in Lebanon, Connecticut, to accept her son as a pupil. (Calvinism is a Protestant branch of Christianity that places strong emphasis on the supreme power of God, the sinfulness of mankind, and the doctrine of predestination, which states that all human events are controlled by God.) Although Occom's health was fragile and he was susceptible to eyestrain, he entered a life that required extensive reading and frequent preaching tours. After he began studying with Wheelock, he was driven by the desire to learn how to read so he could study the Bible (the holy book of the Christian religion). His stay with Wheelock eventually extended into the late 1740s. Before Occom had completed his studies, Wheelock sent him to preach to the Montauks, who lived on the eastern tip of Long Island. The prior minister of the Montauk people had decided to move west and preach to the Shinnecocks.

Ministry brings hardship

The Montauks encouraged Occom to extend his stay with them. In 1751, against the objections of Wheelock, Occom married one of his students, Mary Fowler. The Occoms

Eleazar Wheelock

Best known today as the founder of Dartmouth College, Eleazar Wheelock was Native American preacher Samson Occom's instructor. Born in New Haven, Connecticut, he graduated from Yale College in 1733. Two years later he was appointed pastor of a Congregational church in Lebanon, Connecticut. While living in Lebanon, Wheelock became interested in the education of Native Americans, and in 1754 he opened a school that relied on the charity of Europeans and the church to educate Native American students. One of his first students was Occom, who proved to be an enthusiastic learner and a devout Christian. Wheelock sent Occom to England to solicit funds to support the mission of educating and converting Native Americans. After accumulating 50,000 dollars, Wheelock moved the charity school to present-day Hanover, New Hampshire, and reopened it as Dartmouth College in 1770. This development, among other incidents, caused Occom to question the depth of Wheelock's commitment to Native Americans. Wheelock was the first president of Dartmouth, and he helped the institution survive the difficult years of the Revolutionary War (1775–83), in which the American colonies won their independence from Great Britain.

had ten children, and the marriage lasted until Occom's death. Despite his being a loving husband and father, the family was never financially secure. The annual salary Occom received from the Boston Commissioners, who oversaw religious affairs, was only fifteen pounds (a pound is a British monetary unit). Occom received none of the assistance generally given to English clergymen and teachers. As a result he soon had a debt of more than fifty pounds. The Occoms had to purchase their own wood and raise their own corn, but they were not allowed to keep sheep. When Samson was away preaching, Mary often had to beg for money from Wheelock and others in order to buy food and necessities. Church leaders claimed, however, that the Occoms were poor simply because they did not know how to budget their money.

Poverty plagued Occom all his life. He felt he was being treated differently because of his race—particularly after he was ordained (officially appointed with ministerial or priestly authority) in 1759 and learned that another young minister was granted 180 pounds annually. That year Occum was considered for a ministry among the Cherokees in the South, but he was prevented from taking the position when the Cherokees illegally invaded English settlers' territory. Occom's physical labors, meanwhile, further affected his health. During this time, for instance, he suffered from bleeding ulcers (open sores) of the thigh. Yet he continued visiting the Montauks and other tribes, preaching as opportunities arose. Occom once ventured into New York City and Yonkers, but he was appalled at the loose moral standards among the colonists. After preaching to the Oneidas in 1761, he was given a wampum (beads used by Native Americans as money, ceremonial pledges, and ornaments) belt signifying a bond of friendship. Over the next three decades Occum frequently returned to minister to the Oneidas.

Joins Wheelock's charity school

In 1754 Wheelock established his Indian charity school. His mission was to prepare young Native Americans for a life of "light in pure truth," the central doctrine of Calvinism. Relations between Occum and Wheelock had always fluctuated—primarily because Occum was considered a spendthrift—yet for many years Occom was an effective fund-raiser for the school. By 1764 Iroquois and white charity students had enlarged the student body. The following year Wheelock conceived the idea of sending Occom and the Reverend Daniel Whitaker to England and Scotland on a fund-raising campaign. The circumstances of this journey and Wheelock's intentions regarding the future of the school ultimately eroded Occom's faith in his old teacher. During the tour Occom, who preferred to proceed cautiously, had an uneasy relationship with Whitaker, who was more aggressive and caught up in grand visions. Occum never forgot his Native American identity, and his hosts in England and Scotland showered him with flattery and admiration. Nevertheless, Whitaker reported in a letter to Wheelock that Occom spent money extravagantly and conducted himself in a manner unworthy of a Christian minister.

Involved in Mohegan Land Case

Occom returned from the tour in 1767. Over 50,000 dollars had been collected to support Wheelock's mission of educating and converting young Native Americans. At this time, however, Occum learned that Wheelock planned to change the charity school to Dartmouth College and move it to present-day Hanover, New Hampshire. Occum objected strenuously to the idea as a "fraudulent diversion of the endowment from the Indians to the whites," and he protested relocating the school in New Hampshire. In addition, Occom came to realize that Wheelock had been patronizing him—

considering him as a successful "creature" rather than a devoted Christian human being. While Occum tried to remain politically independent in affairs affecting Native Americans, he was often drawn into situations and forced to take a position. An example was the Mohegan Land Case, also known as the Mason Controversy. This drawn-out legal conflict resulted from an agreement drafted in 1640. Under the agreement, Major John Mason a commander in the Pequot War and a political leader in Connecticut, granted land to the Mohegans. Nevertheless the Colony of Connecticut sought to claim the land. While the Mohegans trusted Mason and his heirs, the tribe accused the colony of fraud.

For over a century, the Masons, the Mohegans, and the Colony of Connecticut were caught up in complex litigation (contesting the law). By the time Occom returned from preaching to the Montauks in 1764, the Mohegans had broken into factions (separate groups). Occum sympathized with the larger pro-Mason group, who were claiming the land for the Mohegans. Occom's role in the controversy infuriated the Reverend David Jewett, whose church was on Mohegan lands. Jewett issued charges of misconduct, public clamor, and heresy (opinions contrary to the church) against Occom before the Connecticut Board of Correspondence. At a hearing on March 12, 1765, the Board exonerated (cleared from accusation or blame) Occom except for his actual participation in the Mason issue. Heavily influenced by Wheelock, Occum submitted a humble apology for trying to protect his tribe's land claim. Such English cunning against Native Americans distressed Occom, adding to his personal difficulties and causing him to have problems with alcohol.

Gives famous sermon

Throughout his life Occom kept an extensive diary and maintained a written record of his sermons. He delivered his most famous sermon at the execution of Moses Paul, a Native American who was a former soldier and sailor. On a December night in 1771 in Waterbury, Connecticut, Paul was thrown out of a tavern because he was drunk and rowdy. Seeking revenge, he attacked and killed Moses Cook, the first patron to come out of the tavern. After being tried and sentenced to be hanged, Paul gained a three-month reprieve (delay of punishment). He requested that Occom preach a sermon at his execution. Numerous Native Americans were among the clergymen, lawyers, and judges attending the event on a stormy September 2, 1772. All came to witness the execution—the first in New Haven since 1759—and to hear the Native American preacher. Occom found himself in a difficult position: he was expected to urge Native Americans to refrain from drinking alcohol, yet he realized the English used strong drink to weaken the spirit of his people.

Occom began the sermon with quotes from the Bible, warning that humans are sinful by nature. He then addressed Paul, who stood on the gallows (frame where hanging takes place), before speaking to the whites in the audience. He ended with a lengthy speech to Native Americans about the sins of drunkenness. The sermon had an equally lengthy title: *A Sermon, Preached at the Execution of Moses Paul, an Indian; Who Was Executed at New Haven, on the Second of September, 1772; For the Murder of Mr. Moses Cook, Late of Waterbury, on the 7th of December, 1771. Preached at the Desire of Said Paul. By Samson Occom. Minister of the Gospel, and Missionary to the Indians.* Occum's sermon has since become a classic in American "gallows literature." First published on October 31, 1772, in New Haven, it was reissued from New London two weeks later. The tenth edition appeared in 1780, and there were several subsequent printings. Later editions reportedly contained an introduction with a faked dialogue between Occum and Paul on the eve of the execution.

Writes hymns

Occom is also known as a writer of hymns. He began to appreciate hymns while studying with Wheelock, and in England he met several hymn writers with whom he carried on a correspondence. The actual number of Occum's compositions is unknown, but many are included in his *Collection of Hymns and Spiritual Songs* (1774). One hymn widely considered to be by Occom is "Awaked by Sinai's Awful Sound," which was published after his death.

Toward the end of his life Occom and his wife settled in the Stockbridge Oneida community in New York. (The Stockbridge Oneida were tribes from the Hudson Valley and westward who became Christian converts and were referred to as "Praying Indians"; see **John Eliot** entry). On July 14, 1792, Occom collapsed while walking back to his house after completing an article. He was found dead by his wife. More than three hundred Native Americans attended his funeral.

For further research

Blodgett, Harold. *Samson Occom.* Hanover, N.H.: Dartmouth College Publications, 1935.

Encyclopedia of North American Indians. New York: Houghton, 1996, pp. 434–36.

James Edward Oglethorpe

December 22, 1696
London, England
July 1, 1785
Essex, England

British general and philanthropist, founder of Georgia colony

James Oglethorpe was an English general and member of Parliament (the British legislative body) who obtained a grant to start a colony for debtors (those who cannot pay their bills). He named this North American colony Georgia. The British Crown (monarchy or royal family) had political reasons for approving the Georgia venture: the colony would serve as a buffer between English-held South Carolina and Florida, which was occupied by Spain, an enemy of Britain. In 1733 Oglethorpe founded the city of Savannah, then set about acquiring land from the friendly Yamacraw tribe and fortifying the town against the Spanish. His tenure as governor in Georgia proved to be controversial. Within two years he had imposed regulations banning rum and slavery in the colony, a move that caused intense opposition from settlers. After England declared war on Spain in 1739, Oglethorpe led a failed expedition against the Spanish town of St. Augustine. Although his successful defense of the colony in 1742 assured its survival, Oglethorpe had financial difficulties and the settlers became restless. In 1743 he was charged with mismanagement and called back to England. Oglethorpe was later

"One, driven by strong benevolence of soul,/ Shall fly like Oglethorpe from pole to pole."

From Imitation of Horace *by English poet Alexander Pope.*

James Edward Oglethorpe (left) negotiating with Native Americans.
Reproduced by permission of The Library of Congress.

exonerated (cleared from accusation or blame), but he never saw his colony again.

Joins army at age fourteen

James Edward Oglethorpe was born in London, England, on December 22, 1696, the third and youngest surviving son of Theophilus and Eleanor (Wall) Oglethorpe. In 1710, when he was only fourteen, he joined the British army. Two years later he volunteered for service in the army of Prince Eugène in Eastern Europe. In 1714 Oglethorpe was admitted to Corpus Christi College at Oxford, and by 1722 he had become a member of the House of Commons (the lower branch of Parliament). Then Oglethorpe's life took a dramatic turn when a friend named Castell died. Castell had been declared a pauper (one who cannot pay debts) and sentenced to Fleet, a debtor's prison. When he was unable to afford the fees required at Fleet, he was placed in a house where the inmates were infected with smallpox (a highly infectious, often fatal, viral disease). Castell soon died of the disease, an event that deeply affected Oglethorpe and inspired him to investigate conditions in debtor's prisons.

Obtains Georgia charter

As a member of the House of Commons, Oglethorpe took the prison issue before Parliament. He was subsequently appointed chairman of a committee charged with determining the reasons for the deplorable state of debtor's prisons. Oglethorpe and his committee discovered extensive corruption among prison officials, who also committed horrible brutalities against inmates. These revelations led Oglethorpe to devote his energies to reforming policies on the treatment of paupers. At the time the traditional remedy for solving a nation's problems was to send undesirable citizens and social misfits to a colony. Acting upon his ideas for prison reform, Oglethorpe gathered twenty like-minded partners and applied for a charter (a contract issued by the English Crown that gave a group of settlers the right to start a colony and establish a government) to settle Georgia (named in honor of King George II), a debtor's colony in America. In 1732 Oglethorpe and his partners were named trustees of the colony and granted a tract of land located between the Savannah and Alatamaha Rivers along the south Atlantic seaboard.

At the same time Oglethorpe anonymously published an essay in which he solicited funds for the Georgia project. His primary purpose was to justify transporting many of England's worst social offenders to form their own community in a strange land. Oglethorpe carefully explained that he anticipated the serious problems that could arise among a group of criminals. His first step, he wrote, would be to place all of the settlers under his own supervision. Since Oglethorpe was a seasoned army officer, there was little question that he would be able to maintain discipline. He also pointed out that poverty would not be the sole requirement for participation in the venture, and he would control the selection of settlers.

The colony had a political purpose as well. In addition to serving as a refuge for paupers, Georgia would provide a barrier against Spain, which had been mounting raids on British settlements along the Atlantic coast. At the time the southernmost English colony was South Carolina. About 250 miles farther south was the heavily fortified Spanish seaport settlement of St. Augustine. Lying between the British and the Spanish was a wilderness frontier. The British proposed to establish Georgia on the frontier, then build forts that would give colonies to the north protection against the Spanish. For military reasons African slavery, which was a vital part of the South Carolina economy, would not be permitted in Georgia. In addition, rum could not be sold to Native Americans by traders in the colony. These prohibitions would later cause problems for Oglethorpe.

Starts colony

Oglethorpe and his trustees received generous funding for the Georgia colony—sizable private contributions were supplemented by 10,000 pounds (a sum of British money) from Parliament. In November 1732, Oglethorpe and 120 settlers sailed for America aboard the ship *Anne*. Oglethorpe immediately located a site for the settlement and built the town of Savannah. (Savannah is now considered one of the most beautiful historic American cities.) His next act was to establish friendly relations with the Yamacraws, the local Native American tribe. The colonists and the Yamacraws maintained a spirit of goodwill throughout Oglethorpe's stay in Georgia, and he was able to purchase more land for the colony from them. Within two years Oglethorpe had opened the colony to settlers other than ex-convicts, mainly German Protestant refugees and Highlanders (people who live in hilly or mountainous areas) from Scotland. New settlements expanded westward, and about sixty miles south of Savannah the town of Frederica was built on an island at the mouth of the Alatamaha River.

Discord begins

In 1734 Oglethorpe went back to England, accompanied by several Native American chiefs. Before he left he appointed a prominent shopkeeper as an interim supervisor of the colony. The choice was a disaster, revealing Oglethorpe's poor judgment and exposing just how difficult it was to manage such an unusual settlement. Some historians have observed that Georgia, a small colony, was organized on a community plan that functioned only if all of the inhabitants did their jobs and followed the rules. Moreover, Oglethorpe was a firm ruler who attended to even the smallest details himself. Not only did the shopkeeper turn out to be a dishonest and brutal man, as acting supervisor he was unable to keep order. Colonists were not interested in being good citizens, and he had difficulty enforcing the ban on rum and slave trade. When Oglethorpe returned he was welcomed by near chaos. He dismissed the interim supervisor, but the colonists continued to be disgruntled about not being able to trade in rum and slaves.

Unrest also resulted from the influence of Methodism (a Protestant religious group). John Wesley and Charles Wesley, whom Oglethorpe had invited to the colony, arrived in 1736; Charles was appointed Oglethorpe's private secretary and his brother John as head of missionary activities. Charles and Oglethorpe soon had a disagreement, however, and Charles returned to England after only a brief stay in Georgia. John Wesley remained, but his presence was a source of turmoil and discontent. While Oglethorpe was preparing a defense against Spain, John Wesley quarreled with other officials. Then Oglethorpe decided to replace Wesley with the popular evangelical preacher **George Whitefield** (see entry), who arrived in November 1739. Whitefield improved the situation somewhat by starting an orphanage, which he called Bethesda, on five hundred acres of land granted to him by the Georgia trustees. He was so dictatorial (oppressive or overbearing to others), however, that he alienated the guardians of the orphans. Finally, after a five-month stay, Whitefield left in April 1740 to continue his preaching tour, which sparked the religious revival called the "Great Awakening."

Heroically defends Georgia

While Oglethorpe was losing control of his colony, he took command on the military front. War between Spain and Britain was ready to begin at any time, and Oglethorpe knew that Georgia would become the field of battle. He received word that St. Augustine residents were being evacuated from their homes to accommodate a Spanish troop buildup. In September 1738 Oglethorpe raised a volunteer army of six hundred men, among them troops from South Carolina. Then in the summer of 1739 he led his regiment through the wilderness toward St. Augustine. Along the way he formed an alliance with several Native American tribes, accumulating a force of two thousand. By fall England had declared war on Spain, and the following spring Oglethorpe mounted an attack on St. Augustine. Although he succeeded in capturing three Spanish forts, he was not able to seize St. Augustine itself. In the heat of battle many Native American warriors left because they did not approve of Oglethorpe's fighting style. Also, sickness broke out and many Carolina soldiers deserted. In June 1740 Oglethorpe withdrew his troops. Nevertheless his efforts had been effective because the Spanish did not venture into Georgia for two years.

In 1742 the Spanish bombarded British defenses around Georgia. During his defense of the colony Oglethorpe achieved the victory for which he is remembered today. Although his forces were not prepared for the attack, Oglethorpe led them into battle and brilliantly fought off the Spanish invaders. At one point he even captured two Spanish soldiers single-handedly. Soon English ships sailed to the colonists' rescue, and Georgia remained intact. Yet Oglethorpe's difficulties were not over. The British government would not give him enough funds for military defense, so over the following year he had to rely on Native American allies to

James Oglethorpe and his Chickasaw allies during the Spanish attack on the English colony of Georgia.
Reproduced by permission of The Granger Collection.

conduct raids into Spanish territory. Finally, Oglethorpe began using his own money to buy supplies and other necessities for the militia. Internal conflict was still brewing, however, and colonists complained about his rigid policies. Oglethorpe was recalled to England and charged with mismanagement. In an attempt to sort out his financial situation he submitted a bill to the British government. Although charges against him were eventually dropped, officials did not refund his money, saying the expenses had not been authorized.

Lives final years in England

Oglethorpe intended to return to Georgia, but he never saw his colony again. In 1743 he married Elizabeth Wright, a wealthy heiress who owned Cranham Hall, a large estate in Essex. Two years later he was involved in an insurrection (revolt against an established government), an act that led to his being court-martialed (tried by a military court) for treason. He was acquitted but his military career was over. When the Georgia trustees surrendered their patent in 1752, the colony was taken over by the royal government. Oglethorpe, however, continued to serve in Parliament until 1754, becoming a prominent member of London society. He lived for forty-two years at Cranham Hall, where he died in 1785, at age eighty-nine.

For further research

Blackburn, Joyce. *James Edward Oglethorpe*. New York: Dodd, Mead, 1970.

Spaulding, Phinizy. *Oglethorpe in America*. Athens, Ga.: University of Georgia Press, 1984.

Stephen, Leslie, and Sidney Lee, eds. *The Dictionary of National Biography*. London, England: Oxford University Press, 1917, pp. 937–43.

William Penn

October 14, 1644
London, England
July 30, 1718
Berkshire, England

Founder of Pennsylvania

"When the purchase was agreed, great promises passed between us of kindness and good neighborhood, and that the Indians and English must live in love, as long as the sun gave light."

William Penn.

William Penn was an English aristocrat (member of the upper social class) who founded the colony of Pennsylvania. Although he was born into the Anglican faith (the Church of England, the official state religion), he became a Quaker as a young man. (See box on Quakerism.) At that time Quakerism was outlawed in England, and Penn served at least three jail terms for practicing his religious beliefs. In 1682 he went to America to establish Pennsylvania as a haven for Quakers and others who experienced religious persecution. The colony was a success, yet Penn himself received no profit from his efforts. In fact, the venture ruined him financially, and toward the end of his life he spent a year in debtor's prison. Moreover, he was constantly engaged in a struggle with colonists who wanted to return control of Pennsylvania to the British monarchy. Today, Penn is remembered for signing one of the few treaties that brought a prolonged peace between Native Americans and European colonists.

Born during time of strife

William Penn was born into a privileged and wealthy family on October 14, 1644, in London, England. His father,

William Penn (1621–1670), was an admiral in the British Royal Navy, and the owner of several large estates in Ireland. He was also a friend of the Stuart kings of England. (The Stuarts were a family who had ruled Scotland and England since the twelfth century.) Penn's mother was Margaret Jasper Vanderschuren, who was the widow of a Dutch merchant before she married Penn's father. In 1641 she and her family fled Ireland for London, England, as Irish Catholics waged a war against Protestant immigrants. In London she met and married William Penn. Their elder son and primary heir, William, was born in 1644, during a time of political unrest. A civil war was raging in England, and the king was being held prisoner in Scotland. There was also religious turmoil. Dissidents (people who disagree with the rules of a government or church) such as George Fox, the founder of the Religious Society of Friends (known as Quakers), were preaching throughout England for religious reform. Penn's father was arrested on suspicion of treason (betraying one's country) because he was a friend of the Stuarts, but he was soon released. In 1654 he headed for the West Indies and became involved in a military assault on the Spanish at Hispaniola. This grand expedition ended in failure, and on his return the older Penn was imprisoned again. Upon his release he decided that England was not safe, so in 1656 he moved the family to Ireland. In 1660 the English civil war came to an end and the Stuarts regained the throne. That same year young William was sent to study at Oxford's Christ Church College.

Becomes a Quaker

William Penn Jr. had his first religious experience at the age of ten or eleven. When he was thirteen he met Thomas Loe, an itinerant (one who travels from place to place) Quaker, who visited Ireland and was invited to the Penn home. This was Penn's first encounter with Quakerism, although it did not then lead to his conversion. At Oxford, Penn realized he needed a more personal religious faith than was provided by the Church of England. In 1662 he was expelled for not attending chapel, which was required of all students. Meanwhile, Quakerism had been outlawed in England. Penn's father then sent him to France, the center of elite society, where he was introduced at the court of King Louis XIV at Fontainebleau. Soon bored with court life, young William enrolled in the Protestant Academy of Saumur, where he stayed for a year and a half.

William Penn concluding
a treaty with the
Delaware tribe.

In 1666 Penn went to Ireland to manage the family estates. The following year he again encountered Loe, and this time he underwent an intense religious awakening. He began attending Quaker meetings and was briefly jailed in Cork because of his actions. (Ireland was part of the British Empire, so Penn was breaking the law when he attended Quaker meetings in Cork.) He also wrote his first public statement against religious intolerance, and at age twenty-four he became a minister. When he held Quaker meetings he was again arrested, imprisoned this time in the Tower of London. While he was in jail he wrote several tracts on religious freedom, the most famous being *No Cross No Crown* (1669). In 1670 Penn's father died, leaving young William not only a substantial fortune but also a large debt owed to the estate by the Stuart kings—a debt that led to the founding of Pennsylvania. After being jailed a third time, Penn left for Europe to spread the word of Quakerism in Germany and Holland. He would later urge German and Dutch converts to settle in Pennsylvania.

Quakerism

As a young man William Penn joined the Religious Society of Friends, commonly called Quakers. "Quaker" was initially an uncomplimentary term used by members of the established church to describe the Friends. Founded in 1668 by English religious leader George Fox, Quakerism contended that an ordained priest and a formal worship service were not needed to establish communion between an individual and God. Fox believed all people were endowed with an "inner light" that enabled them to understand and be guided by the Holy Spirit. Among the early converts to Quakerism were Separatists who had withdrawn from the Church of England, the official state religion, because they considered it corrupt and repressive. The Quakers refused to attend church services and pay tithes (monetary offerings paid to the church). Opponents of violence and war, they would not bear arms or vow allegiance to the government. Quakers also believed in the total equality of men and women, and they refused to remove their hats in the presence of people who were considered to be their superiors—at the time, a very rebellious and disrespectful act.

Quakerism was outlawed in England until the Tolerance Act was passed in 1669. During the late seventeenth century the Quakers sent missionaries to other European countries and to America, Asia, and Africa. Extending their activities to social reform, they were among the first to propose the abolition (end) of slavery. They also campaigned for more humane criminal laws (they opposed capital punishment and the death sentence), improvements in mental institutions, and education for common people. Quakers who settled in America were generally subjected to persecution, but they found refuge in Penn's colony, Pennsylvania, and in Rhode Island, which was founded by **Roger Williams** (see entry) on the principle of religious freedom. Although Quakers in the American colonies remained pacifists (those opposed to war) during the Revolutionary War (1775–83), they were loyal to the new United States government.

Founds Pennsylvania

In 1675 Penn was involved in writing a liberal charter of government for Quakers settling in the American colony of East Jersey (now New Jersey). In 1681 he formed a company with eleven other investors and purchased East Jersey. That same year he also reminded King Charles II of the royal debt that was owed to the Penn estate. Instead of asking to be repaid with money, however, he requested a tract of land north of Maryland in America. Knowing persecution firsthand, Penn planned to establish a colony based on religious and political freedom. After being appointed proprietor of Pennsylvania (named Penn's Woods by Charles II in honor of Penn's father), he arrived in America in 1682. At that time he signed one of the few treaties with the Native Americans that brought about a prolonged peace. He stayed only two years before returning to England to help fellow Quakers fight a renewed round of persecution. He also needed to settle the southern boundary of his colony, which was being claimed by Charles Calvert, Third Lord Baltimore, the governor of Maryland. By this time James II , a Roman Catholic, had become king of England. (Roman Catholicism is a branch of Christianity that is based in Rome, Italy, and headed by a pope who is considered infallible [unable to make a mistake]. The pope oversees all bishops and priests of the church, who are authorized to forgive sins.) James II was overthrown in 1688, however, and the Protestant rulers King William III and Queen Mary II ascended the throne. This turn of events meant trouble for Penn, who no longer had a personal relationship with the monarchy. Since he was still absent from Pennsylvania, he lost his authority there as well. In 1692 the Crown (royal government) withdrew Penn's proprietorship because the Pennsylvania colony was poorly managed during Penn's absence. King William III appointed a new governor, Benjamin Fletcher, who immediately had his own problems. For example, the pacifist Quakers were opposed to using Pennsylvania funds for military purposes. In hopes of compromising with the Quakers the king finally restored the charter to Penn, who returned to Pennsylvania in 1699 only to face growing opposition from settlers who wanted the Crown to take over the colony. Staying for two years, he helped draft the Charter of Privileges (1701), which were legal reforms that gave some power to an elected assembly (elected representatives). But affairs in England called him home. He arrived there in December 1701, never again to see his colony.

Ends life in poverty

Penn spent his final years battling opponents who wanted Pennsylvania to come under English rule. He was also

Penn's treaty with Native Americans

William Penn, the proprietor of Pennsylvania, signed one of the few treaties that brought a prolonged peace between Native Americans and European colonists. In *The Propriety of Pennsylvania* he described the process of forming the treaty with Native American dignitaries:

. . . . *Having thus introduced the matter, he [the representative of the Native American sachem] fell to the bounds of the land they had agreed to dispose of, and the price (which [land] now is little and dear, that which would have bought twenty miles, not buying now two). During this time that this person spoke, not a man of them was observed to whisper or smile; the old, grave, the young, reverent in their deportment; they do speak little, but fervently, and with elegancy. I have never seen more natural sagacity [wisdom], considering them without help (I was a'going to say, the spoil) of tradition; and he will deserve the name of wise, that outwits them in any treaty about a thing they understand.*

When the purchase was agreed, great promises passed between us of kindness and good neighborhood, and that the Indians and English must live in love, as long as the sun gave light. Which done, another made a speech to the Indians, in the name of all the Sachamakers or kings, first to tell them what was done; next, to charge and command them, to love the Christians, and particularly to live in peace with me, and the people under my government; that many governors had been in the river, but that no governor had come himself to live and stay here before; and having now such a one that had treated them well, they should never do him or his any wrong. At every sentence of which they shouted, and said Amen, in their way. . . .

. . . . *We have agreed, that in all differences between us, six of each side shall end the matter. Don't abuse them, but let them have justice, and you will win them. The worst is that they are the worse for the Christians, who have propagated [spread] their vices, and yielded them tradition for ill, and not for good things. . . .*

Reprinted in: Stiles, T. J., ed. In Their Own Words: The Colonizers. *New York: Berkley Publishing Group, 1998.*

confronted with substantial debts that threatened to ruin him. Although the colony had been a success, it had yielded very little profit for Penn. He was also swindled by one of his agents. Crushed by the financial burden, he went to debtor's prison in 1707. Five years later he began negotiating with the Crown for the sale of Pennsylvania, but during these discussions he suffered a series of disabling strokes. He lingered on until 1718, when he finally died. The Pennsylvania colony remained under the control of the Penn family until the American Revolution (1775–83).

For further research

Dolson, Hildegarde. *William Penn, Quaker Hero*. New York: Random House, 1961.

Foster, Genevieve. *The World of William Penn*. New York: Scribner, 1973.

Stiles, T. J., ed. *In Their Own Words: The Colonizers*. New York: Berkley Publishing Group, 1998.

Wildes, Harry Emerson. *William Penn*. New York: Macmillan, 1974.

Eliza Lucas Pinckney

December 28, 1722?
West Indies
May 26, 1793

Plantation manager, indigo cultivator

Eliza Lucas Pinckney was a South Carolina plantation manager who is known today for her pioneering work in the
cultivation of indigo (a plant used to make blue dye). As a
result of Pinckney's successful experiments—which she began
at the age of seventeen—the Carolina colony sustained a flourishing indigo industry for nearly three decades. During her
lifetime Pinckney kept a detailed journal, recording the
progress of her experiments. She also maintained extensive
correspondence with friends and family members. Her letters,
one of the largest surviving collections of letters by a colonial
woman, provide valuable information about Carolina plantation life during the eighteenth century.

Left in charge of plantations

Eliza Lucas Pinckney was born in the West Indies (a
group of islands in the Caribbean Sea) around 1722. Her father,
George Lucas, was a lieutenant colonel in the British Army and
later served as lieutenant governor of Antigua (an island
colony in the West Indies). Pinckney received an excellent
education in England. An accomplished musician, she was

" . . . I was very early
fond of the vegetable
world. . . . "

Eliza Lucas Pinckney.

"fond of the vegetable world"

At the age of seventeen, Eliza Lucas Pinckney began conducting experiments with indigo crops, which resulted in a flourishing indigo industry in the Carolina colony for nearly thirty years. Near the end of her life, in 1785, Pinckney described her indigo experiments in the following letter to one of her children:

My Dear Child

You wish me to inform you what I recollect of the introducing and culture of indigo in this country. You have heard me say I was very early fond of the vegetable world, my father was pleased with it and encouraged it, he told me the turn I had for those amusements might produce something of real and public utility, if I could bring to perfection the plants of other countries which he would procure

me. Accordingly when he went to the West Indies he sent me a variety of seeds, among them the indigo. I was ignorant both of the proper season for sowing it, and the soil best adapted to it. To the best of my recollection I first try'd it in March 1741, or 1742; it was destroyed (I think by a frost). The next time in April, and it was cut down by a worm; I persevered to a third planting and succeeded, and when I informed my father it bore seed and the seed ripened, he sent a man from the Island of Monserat by the name of Cromwell who had been accustomed to making indigo there, and gave him high wages; he made some brick vats on my fathers plantation on Wappo Creek and then made the first indigo; it was very indifferent, and he made a great mistery of it, said he repented coming as he should ruin his own country by it, for my father had engaged him to let me see the whole

especially talented at playing the flute. She also spoke French, and her father encouraged her to read widely. Pinckney once noted in her diary: "I have a little library well furnished for my papa has left me most of his books." She delved into the works of such authors as John Locke, Virgil, and Plutarch, and she even showed an interest in the legal writings of Thomas Wood.

In 1738 Pinckney's mother, whose name is not known, became ill. Seeking a more healthful climate, Lucas moved the family to a plantation he had inherited on Wappoo (also Wappo) Creek in South Carolina, near present-day Charleston. When the War of Jenkins' Ear (1739–41; a naval conflict between England and Spain) broke out the following year, Lucas returned to his military post in Antigua. Since her mother was ailing and her father was away, Pinckney—as the eldest of four children—was left in charge of Wappoo planta-

process. I observed him as carefully as I could and informed Mr. Deveaux an old gentleman a neighbour of ours of the little knowledge I had gain'd and gave him notice when the indigo was to be beat; he saw and afterwards improved upon it, not withstanding the churlishness [rudeness] of Cromwell, who wished to deceive him, and threw in so large a quantity lime water as to spoil the colour. In the year 1744 I married, and my father made Mr. Pinckney [Charles Pinckney, her husband] a present of all the indigo then upon the ground as the fruit of my industry. The whole was saved for seed, and your father gave part of it away in small quantities to a great number of people that year, the rest he planted the next year at Ashipo for seed, which he sold, as did some of the gentlemen to whom he had given it the year before; by this means there soon became plenty in the country. Your father gained all the information he could from the French prisoners brought in here, and used every other means of information, which he published in the Gazette for the information of the people at large.

The next year Mr. Cattle sent me a present of a couple of large plants of the wild indigo which he had just discovered. Experiments were afterwards made upon this sort, which proved to be good indigo, but it did not produce so large a quantity as the cultivated sort. I am

Your truly affectionate mother,

Eliza Pinckney

Reprinted in: Kupperman, Karen Ordahl, ed. Major Problems in American Colonial History. Lexington, Mass.: D. C. Heath and Company, 1993, pp. 320–21.

tion. She was also responsible for running two other family plantations in the area. Pinckney was only seventeen years old.

Experiments with indigo

Pinckney approached her new responsibilities with enthusiasm. Maintaining a steady correspondence with her father, she relied on his advice on agricultural matters. He encouraged her to try several different crops at Wappoo. In 1739 she noted in her diary that she was particularly interested in cultivating indigo: "Wrote my Father . . . On the pains I had taken to bring the Indigo, Ginger, Cotton and Lucerne and Casada to perfection and had greater hopes from the Indigo (if I could have the seed earlier next year from the West India's [sic]) than any of the rest of the things I had tryd."

Pinckney apparently realized that indigo would benefit the colony of South Carolina for two reasons. First, the plant could be used to make blue dye-cakes that would be sold to cloth manufacturers in England. At the time English textile (cloth) makers had to buy indigo dye from the French West Indies, a fact that they resented. Therefore, securing a direct supply from Carolina, which was then an English colony, would solve the problem of having to rely on the French. Second, an indigo crop would replace the declining rice market, traditionally the main product of Carolina. The war in Europe had disrupted the demand for rice, however, and the Carolina economy was now suffering.

Pinckney probably knew that her experiments with indigo might not succeed. The cultivation of indigo had been tried near Charleston seventy years earlier, but all efforts had met with failure. She was therefore taking a risk, especially since, as she recalled later in life, she was "ignorant both of the proper season for sowing it [indigo] and the soil best adapted to it." Lucas continued sending his daughter indigo seeds from Antigua. In the summer of 1741 he hired Nicholas Cromwell, an experienced indigo maker from the French island of Montserrat, who came to Wappoo to show Pinckney how to make dye. The following October, she reported to her father that she and Cromwell had made "20 weight of Indigo" and she requested "a hundred weight of seed to plant in the spring."

Pinckney soon realized that she and her father had placed too much trust in Cromwell. He did not want Carolina to compete with Montserrat for the indigo trade, so he poured lime water on Pinckney's indigo and ruined the color of the dye. Not to be discouraged, Lucas sent Patrick Cromwell, another indigo expert and the brother of Nicholas, to Wappoo. With the assistance of the more honest Cromwell, Pinckney continued her experiments for three years. Finally, in 1744, she had a successful crop.

Indigo trade booms

While Pinckney was perfecting her indigo crops she also pursued other interests. She was a tutor for her sister, and she taught two young black female servants to read so they could become "school mistress's for the rest of the Negroe chil-

dren." In 1741 Pinckney observed a comet whose appearance had been predicted by English astronomer Isaac Newton. In 1744, at the age of twenty-two, she married Charles Pinckney, a widower and family friend who was in his mid-forties. The first licensed lawyer native to Carolina, he had been speaker of the Commons House of Assembly (the Carolina legislative body). After they were married Charles Pinckney sent six pounds of his wife's indigo dye to English cloth manufacturers, who declared it to be superior to the French product. He then distributed seed from her crop to planters in the area. By 1746 Carolina was shipping nearly 40,000 pounds of indigo to England. The following year shipments more than doubled, to 100,000 pounds. For the next thirty years the Carolina economy remained prosperous through the sale of indigo. Trade ceased only when the Revolutionary War (1775–83) began and the American colonies declared their independence from Great Britain.

The winding of silk. Eliza Pinckney followed the same process on her plantation.
Reproduced by permission of Corbis-Bettmann.

Plantation manager once again

The Pinckneys had a happy marriage. They built a grand house on the waterfront in Charleston and also lived at Charles's plantation on the Cooper River. At the plantation Eliza raised silkworms and privately manufactured silk. By 1749 she had given birth to four children, one of whom lived for only a short time. In 1753, when Charles was appointed commissioner of the Carolina colony, the Pinckneys moved to London, England. They stayed for five years until war broke out between England and France. Leaving their two sons, Charles Jr. and Thomas, at school in England, they returned with their daughter, Harriot, to South Carolina.

In the summer of 1758 Charles Sr. died of malaria (a disease caused by parasites in the red blood cells). Once again Eliza was left with the responsibility of running a plantation. In addition she managed several other plots of land her husband had owned in the area. During the Revolutionary War, Pinckney's sons came back from England to support the cause of American independence. After the war both entered public service and ran their own plantations. During her later years Pinckney lived with Harriot, who was also widowed, helping to raise her numerous grandchildren. In 1791 Pinckney met George Washington as he was touring the South. Two years later, upon being stricken with cancer, she traveled to Philadelphia, Pennsylvania, to seek a cure. Pinckney died soon thereafter and was buried in Philadelphia. One of the pallbearers at her funeral was Washington.

For further research

"Eliza Lucas Pinckney." http://wwwnetsrq.com/_dbois/pinckney.html Available July 13, 1999.

James, Edward T., and others, eds. *Notable American Women,* Volume III. Cambridge, Mass.: Belknap Press of Harvard University Press, 1971, pp. 69–71.

Kupperman, Karen Ordahl, ed. *Major Problems in American Colonial History.* Lexington, Mass.: D. C. Heath and Company, 1993, pp. 320–21.

Lee, Susan. *Eliza Pinckney.* Chicago: Children's Press, 1977.

Pinckney, Eliza, ed. *The Letterbook of Eliza Lucas Pinckney.* Columbia, S.C.: University of South Carolina Press, 1997.

Pocahontas

1595
Virginia
March 1617
Gravesend, England

**Powhatan-Renapé "princess" who
helped the Virginia colonists**

The story of Pocahontas, a Powhatan-Renapé "princess," is one of the earliest and most deeply rooted legends of American history. According to the legend, Pocahontas saved **John Smith** (see entry), one of the founders of the Virginia Colony, from being executed by her father, **Powhatan** (see entry). If the story is true, Pocahontas may have decisively influenced the course of English settlement in the New World (a European term for North America and South America). Her friendly and generous relationship with Smith and the English settlers helped preserve the colony through the long winters when the colonists were threatened with starvation. With the benefit of hindsight, many Native Americans have criticized her for preventing Powhatan from killing off the colonists. Had she not done so, they say, the English might never have colonized North America and many Native American cultures might have been preserved from extinction (no longer existing). On the other hand, Americans of European descent regard Pocahontas as a savior of their own race and a foremother of the United States.

" . . . I will bee for ever
and ever your
Countrieman. . . . "

Pocahontas.

Portrait: Pocahontas.
*Reproduced by permission
of the International
Portrait Gallery.*

257

Official Souvenir
Jamestown Exposition 1907.

Pocahontas Saving the Life of John Smith.

PAINTING ONLY COPYRIGHTED 1907 BY JAMESTOWN A & S CO

Pocahontas saving the life of John Smith.
Reproduced by permission of Archive Photos, Inc.

Pocahontas saves Smith?

Most of the existing information about Pocahontas's early life comes from the writings of Smith, an English adventurer with the Virginia Company. The company had been licensed by King James I of England to explore the coast of North America and exploit its natural resources. In May 1607 Smith and his party established the settlement of Jamestown, named after the king, on the shores of the James River in present-day Virginia, near Chesapeake Bay. Initially the progress of the settlement was thwarted by jealousy and disagreement among the leaders. Smith himself was imprisoned for some time for insubordination (disobedience to authority). In December 1607, Smith embarked on an expedition up the Chickahominy River, exploring the region for new Native American trading partners, places to prospect for gold, and possible access to the Pacific Ocean. He apparently went too close to a treasure house belonging to Powhatan, the chief of the local Powhatan group, which was part of the

Algonquin tribe. Powhatan's agents captured Smith and took him before the chief.

In a letter to Queen Anne (wife of James I), dated 1616, Smith claimed that Powhatan sentenced him to death. Then, Smith declared, "at the minute of my execution, [Pocahontas] . . . hazarded the beating out of her own braines to save mine." Writing about himself in the third person, Smith gave a fuller account of the event in his *Generall Historie of Virginia* (1624). He wrote that Powhatan fed him well, but then "two great stones were brought before Powhatan: then as many [of the Indians] as could layd hands on him [Smith], dragged him to them, and thereon laid his head, and being ready with their clubs, to beate out his braines, Pocahontas the Kings dearest daughter, when no intreaty could prevaile, got his head in her armes, and laid her owne [u]pon his to sa[v]e him from death."

Is the story true?

Some modern historians have questioned Smith's version of the events that took place in Powhatan's camp. They believe that Smith, a self-promoter, created the story of Pocahontas to enhance his own prestige. In fact, in Smith's earliest description of his meeting with Powhatan, he mentions neither Pocahontas nor an execution. According to an account Smith wrote only a year after the incident, he was brought before Powhatan and the king questioned him about the presence of English settlers in Native American territory. After Smith gave his reply, Powhatan simply sent him back to Jamestown. On the other hand, nothing in Smith's story of Pocahontas can be disproved. For instance, when young Native American men were initiated into full membership in a tribe, they often went through a ceremony that involved a mock execution like the one Smith described. At some point during the execution a sponsor had to speak up for the young man. If this was Smith's initiation ceremony, then Pocahontas served as Smith's sponsor in the tribe. This interpretation makes her later assistance to the English colonists more understandable.

"the willful one"

According to historical documents, Pocahontas seems to have earned her name, "the willful one." Smith believed

Powhatan indulged her and refused her nothing. William Strachey, the official secretary and historian for the Jamestown Colony, called Pocahontas "a well featured but wanton young girle." He added that she frequently engaged in provocative (tending to excite or provoke) behavior: When she was about the age of "11 or 12 yeares, [she would come to the fort and] gett the boyes [to go] forth with her into the markett place and make them wheele [turn handsprings], falling on their hands turning their heeles upwardes, whome she would follow, and wheele so her self naked as she was all the fort over." The spectacle of an unclothed, preteenage girl turning handsprings in such a public place did not fit English ideas of ladylike behavior.

Saves colonists' lives

It is a documented fact that Pocahontas saved the English colonists from starvation. During the early months of 1608, after their own stores and homes burned down, she supplied them with food. Smith recalled, "Now ever once in foure or five dayes, Pocahontas with her attendants brought him [Smith] so much provision, that saved many of their lives, that els for all this had starved." He continued: "James towne with her wild traine she as freely frequented, as her father's habitation, and during the time of two or three yeeres, she next under God, was still the instrument to preserve this Colonie from death, famine and utter confusion; which if in those times, [fit] had once been dissolved, Virginia might have [lain] . . . as it was at our first arrivall to this day."

Acts as negotiator

Pocahontas also served as a go-between for negotiations between her father and the English settlers. In April 1608, one of Smith's fellow captains of the Virginia Company had made the mistake of giving Powhatan tribesmen English steel swords in exchange for turkeys. When Smith refused to barter (trade) any more of his limited supply of weapons, the Powhatans began ambushing settlers and taking their swords, guns, axes, spades, and shovels. Smith then seized seven Powhatan hostages, who confessed that they were acting under their leaders's orders. In mid-May 1608 Powhatan sent Pocahontas to Smith as a negotiator, and Smith finally released his captives to her.

Despite Pocahontas's efforts, relations between her father and the colonists deteriorated. Powhatan was alarmed by the arrival of more colonists and believed that the English intended to take his land away from him. An attempted coronation (crowning) of Powhatan according to English rituals (a plan concocted by Virginia Company officials in London in the hope to gain Powhatan as an ally by making him think he was equal to their own king) did nothing to ease his suspicions. In the autumn of 1608, Powhatan finally forbade all trade with the English. Faced with another hard winter on inadequate rations, Smith decided to confront Powhatan at his capitol, Werowocomoco, and force him to trade under threat of war. In January 1609, Smith and Powhatan met on the banks of the Pamunkey River. According to Smith, Powhatan's major concern was when the English would be leaving: "Some doubt I have," Smith quotes him as saying, "of your comming hither, that makes me not so kindly seeke to relieve you as I would: for many doe informe, your comming hither is not for trade, but to invade my people, and possesse my Country."

Pocahontas again to the rescue

Recognizing that Smith did not intend to leave without the grain he needed, Powhatan decided to remove himself and his family—including Pocahontas—to the town of Orapaks, about fifty miles from Jamestown. Smith and his men were subsequently stranded at Werowocomoco when the barge they had brought to transport the grain was grounded by low tide. They were forced to spend the night in the partly deserted town. In the meantime Powhatan had made plans to attack and kill the English party. Smith and his men were saved once again by Pocahontas, who warned them of her father's intentions and told then to flee. Smith described the event in his *Generall Historie*: "For Pocahontas [Powhatan's] dearest jewell and daughter, in that darke night came through the irksome woods, and told our Captaine [Smith] . . . if we would live, shee wished us presently to be gone."

Smith tried to reward Pocahontas with some trinkets, but she refused the gifts. She feared that Powhatan would punish her if he found out what she had done. Smith wrote: "Such things as shee delighted in, he would have given her: but with the teares running downe her cheekes, shee said shee durst not be seene to have any: for if Powhatan should know it, she were but dead, and so she ranne away by her seffe as she came." Smith did not see Pocahontas again for about eight years. During that time Powhatan and his people ceased trade with the English.

At this point Pocahontas largely drops out of the history of the Jamestown colony. Evidence suggests that she helped hide occasional fugitives who fell into Powhatan's hands, sending them back to the settlement. Smith himself suffered a serious wound—some gunpowder contained in a pouch at his side exploded, stripping the flesh off one leg—and he went back to England in September 1609. He arrived there to find that several men he had exiled from Jamestown for various offenses had returned to England and had levied countercharges against him. He was required to give answers in London. Meanwhile Pocahontas assumed Smith was dead, and since her father had severed ties with the English, she never returned to Jamestown.

Lives with Patawamakes

According to English records, in 1610 Pocahontas married one of her father's supporters, a man named Kocoum. He may have been a member of another tribe, possibly the Patawamakes, who lived farther north on the shores of the Potomac River. Whether for this or some other reason, by 1613 Pocahontas had left her father's territory and was living with friends among the Patawamakes.

Meanwhile in Jamestown, Smith's position was largely taken over by a sea captain named Samuel Argall. The colonists were still suffering from the trading sanctions (prohibiting of trade with his tribe) imposed by Powhatan. The chief had also been waging a guerilla war (a type of unplanned, or unconventional, warfare that involves surprise attacks) against the English for years and taking captives. In late December 1612, while looking for new trading partners, Argall made contact with the chief of the Patawamakes, a man named Iapazaws. When Argall learned that Pocahontas was living with the Patawamakes, he theorized that Powhatan might agree to resume trade if he knew his daughter was being held captive by his enemies. Argall therefore coaxed Pocahontas on board his ship and sailed off with her to Jamestown.

Refuses to rejoin Powhatan

Even though the Englishmen were holding Pocahontas, their negotiations with the Powhatans did not go smoothly. Powhatan was willing to release his English hostages, but he would not give up the guns, swords, and tools he had seized. He claimed they had been stolen from him. Powhatan conducted most of his negotiations through his brother and successor, Opechancanough, who distrusted the English and was ready to fight them. Following an attack by Opechancanough, Argall and acting Jamestown governor Thomas Dale brought Pocahontas on shore to conduct negotiations with the Powhatans. She refused to meet with her father's representatives, choosing instead to remain with the English. According to a letter by Dale quoted in *Purchas his Pilgrimes,* Pocahontas "would not talke to any of [the Powhatans] . . . , [claiming] that if her father had loved her, he would not value her lesse then old Swords, Peeces [guns], or Axes: wherefore shee should still dwell with the English men, who loved her."

Marries John Rolfe

At least one Englishman did love Pocahontas. His name was **John Rolfe** (see entry), and he had come to Jamestown to grow tobacco. (Tobacco was the colony's first successful cash crop, and the basis for the Virginian economy for nearly the next three hundred years.) A devout Christian, Rolfe had courted the captive princess while she was in the care of the Reverend Alexander Whitaker at Henrico, a new community near Jamestown. Whitaker presided at Pocahontas's baptism when she took the name "Rebecca" as a sign of her conversion to Christianity. Rolfe carefully considered his position. He then wrote a lengthy letter to Dale, stating his desire to marry Pocahontas "for the good of the Plantacon, the honor of or Countrye, for the glorye of God, for myne owne salvacon." Both Dale and Powhatan ultimately approved the union. Pocahontas and Rolfe were married at Jamestown in April 1614, a union that spurred the Peace of Pocahontas—a friendship between the English and Powhatan tribes that lasted for many years.

Honored by English royalty

The young couple prospered for three years. In the winter or early spring of 1615, Pocahontas bore Rolfe a son named Thomas. The London owners of the Virginia Company, recognizing that the colony owed its survival to the princess, voted to award her an annual pension for the rest of her life. In addition, they decided to bring her and her family to England to be presented to the king and queen, and to serve as a living advertisement for the company's success. In 1616 the Rolfes sailed for London, accompanied by Dale, who had retired, and Powhatan's representative Uttamatamakin (also Tomocomo). Pocahontas was soon the talk of the town. She met Queen Anne and was later received by King James I. Rolfe did not share in the honor, however, partly because the king was upset with Rolfe for marrying a foreign princess without his permission. Also James did not approve of Rolfe's association with tobacco, a plant the king despised.

Pocahontas's health fails

Pocahontas apparently enjoyed court life. However, in the late winter or early spring of 1616–17, her health began to fail. Rolfe moved her from London to the village of Brentford outside the city. At Brentford, Smith came into her life again. He visited and, "after a modest salutation," Smith wrote, "without any word she turned about, obscured her face, as not seeming well contented." Several hours later Pocahontas regained her composure and confronted Smith: "Were you not afraid to come into my fathers Countrie, and caused feare in him and all his people (but mee), and feare you here I should call you father. I tell you then I will, and you shall call me childe, and so I will bee for ever and ever your Countrieman. . . . They did tell us alwaies you were dead, and I knew no other till I came to Plimouth." Historians speculate that by this statement Pocahontas meant that she would not have married Rolfe had she known Smith was still alive.

The Rolfes embarked for Virginia in mid-March 1617. By that time, however, Pocahontas was critically ill, probably with tuberculosis (a bacterial infection of the lungs) or pneumonia. She was able to travel only as far as Gravesend, toward the mouth of the Thames River. She died there and was buried on March 21, 1617. She was twenty-two years old. The site of her grave has since been lost. John Rolfe returned to Virginia, where he married for a third time. In 1622 Pocahontas's uncle Opechancanough launched a full-fledged massacre of the English, killing about a quarter of the Jamestown population. Rolfe died in the fighting.

For further research

Barbour, Philip L. *Pocahontas and Her World*. Boston: Houghton Mifflin, 1969.

Bataille, Gretchen M., ed. *Native American Women*. New York: Garland Publishing, 1993.

Holler, Anne. *Pocahontas: Powhatan Peacemaker*. Broomal, Pa.: Chelsea House Publishers, 1996.

Hudson, Margaret. *Pocahontas*. Portsmouth, N.H.: Heinemann, 1998.

James, Edward T., and others, eds. *Notable American Women*, Volume III. Cambridge, Mass.: Belknap Press of Harvard University Press, 1971, pp. 78–81.

Pocahontas: Jamestown Rediscovery. http://www.apva.org/history/pocahont.html Available July 13, 1999.

Pocahontas: Savior or Savage? http://theweboftime.com/Poca/POCAHO_l.html Available July 13, 1999.

Shaughnessy, Diane. *Pocahontas: Powhatan Princess*. New York: The Rosen Publishing Group Inc., 1997.

Pontiac

c. 1714
Ohio
April 20, 1769
Cahokia, Illinois

Ottawa-Chippewa tribal leader

Pontiac was an Ottawa chief who led the Pontiac Rebellion in 1763, an attack inspired by Native American resentment at European settlers seizing their land. It was the most impressive Native American resistance movement ever encountered by Europeans in North America. Yet the Pontiac Rebellion failed, primarily because the great chief was unable to form an alliance with the French against the British. Pontiac's war was also significant because Native Americans never again had an opportunity to drive back European settlers. Native tribes continued to lose their land as they were pushed westward and their way of life was totally destroyed.

Trained as Ottawa warrior

Although little is known about Pontiac's youth, it is believed he was born around 1714 along the Maumee River in present-day Ohio, to an Ottawa father and a Chippewa mother. The exact meaning of the name Pontiac has never been determined, but in nineteenth-century Ottawa traditional stories he was called Obwandiyag (pronounced Bwondiac). The English spelled his name "Pontiac," probably

Portrait: Pontiac.

because it sounded that way to them. At the time of Pontiac's birth the Ottawa nation was located at Michilimackinac, on Saginaw Bay, and along the Detroit River. This area is now known as the Great Lakes region. Even though there are no records of Pontiac's life, it is assumed that during his childhood and young adult years he was trained as an Ottawa warrior. As a boy he was probably taught skills that enabled him to hunt and to survive in the woods.

Pontiac was probably also encouraged to utilize weapons and tools introduced by European settlers. At this time the Ottawas and other tribes enjoyed a beneficial relationship with the French, trading their furs for weapons and other goods. Through these transactions, the Ottawa gradually replaced their bows and arrows with guns, which soon became the primary means of obtaining food and ensuring protection. As Pontiac's influence and prosperity increased, he may have had more than one wife and several children. It is known that he had at least one wife, Kantuckeegan, and two sons, Otussa and Shegenaba.

Decides to expel British

After Pontiac rose to a position of power in the Ottawa nation, he was at first inclined to be as friendly to English settlers as he was to French traders. He changed his attitude, however, when he realized that the English were not interested in maintaining good relations with Native Americans. In particular, Pontiac took exception to policies established by Jeffrey Amherst, the British military commander in America. One particularly damaging order prohibited the British from trading gunpowder and ammunition to Native Americans, who had become highly dependent on European weapons. The British were also increasingly intent on taking over Native American land rather than simply establishing military and trading posts. Moreover, the British discontinued the practice of extending credit to Native Americans. Credit had become particularly important because Native peoples often needed European supplies to survive the winter. When spring arrived, they would repay their debts with furs. Pontiac, as well as other leaders, also resented the fact that the British treated Native Americans as if they were a costly inconvenience.

By 1763 Native Americans in the entire Great Lakes region were ready to rebel against British authority. Pontiac

Pontiac (right) holding out a peace pipe to British colonists. Pontiac initially tried to make peace with the colonists, but changed his mind when he learned the British were not interested maintaining good relations with Native Americans.
Reproduced by permission of The Library of Congress.

believed that if the tribes presented a united front and gained support from the French, the British could be forced from Native American territory. His objective was to mount a simultaneous surprise attack on all British forts and settlements. In an effort to achieve his goal, Pontiac sent red wampum (beads used by American Indians as money, ceremonial pledges, and ornaments) belts to Native American tribes from Lake Ontario to the Mississippi River, calling them together in a alliance that would wage the massive assault on the British. Among the tribes that joined Pontiac's initial efforts were the Senecas, Delawares, Shawnees, Miamis, Ottawas, Ojibwas, and Missisaugas. Pontiac's principal target was Detroit, the most important fort in the Great Lakes region. In April 1763 Pontiac outlined his strategy in a speech to three Native American villages—Potawatomi, Ottawa, and Wyandot. He called for the eviction of the British and a return to a traditional lifestyle. His speech rallied the warriors to action.

The Delaware Prophet

By 1763 Native Americans in the Great Lakes region were seething with agitation over the encroachment of English settlers onto their land. The great Ottawa chief Pontiac believed that if the tribes formed an alliance and gained support from the French, the British could be forced from Native American territory. Pontiac's plan may have been influenced by a religious leader known as the Delaware Prophet (also called Neolin). The Delaware Prophet advocated rejection of the European way of life and a return to traditional Native American customs. He depicted the hazards of associating with Europeans by creating a series of deerskin paintings. The pictures illustrate the ways in which white men impeded the Native American way of life. They also portrayed the sins Native Americans had acquired as a result of their contact with white men. While these images had a profound effect on the Great Lakes tribes, they were divided over how to resolve the problem. In his teachings, the Delaware Prophet advocated relinquishing dependence on the European guns. Other Native Americans—including Pontiac—viewed armed conflict as the only way to sever the connection with British settlers. Pontiac's view prevailed, but the resulting rebellion of 1763 eventually led to the total loss of Native American lands.

Pontiac's Rebellion begins

On May 7, 1763, Pontiac put his plan into effect. He would approach Detroit under the pretense of holding a council with the British, then gain access to the fort. Once inside the fort he would give the attack signal to his warriors, who had their weapons hidden under blankets. Pontiac's strategy was destined for failure, however. Reports of the rebellion had already reached Amherst who, in turn, had sent reinforcements to Detroit. When Pontiac saw that the commander at Detroit was prepared for the attack, he decided against giving the prearranged signal and instead ordered a retreat. Despite the presence of heavy British reinforcements, however, Pontiac's warriors were eager for battle. To appease his followers, the chief therefore returned to the fort two days later and launched a strike, but the Native American forces easily went down to defeat.

As the massive revolt continued elsewhere in the Great Lakes region, other tribes had greater success. By June 1 warriors had killed or captured all the inhabitants of Fort Sandusky, Fort St. Joseph, Fort Miami, and Fort Quiatenon. An Ojibwa surprise attack at Michilimackinac on June 2 was probably the most effective conflict of Pontiac's war. During a fake game of lacrosse (a field sport played with sticks and a ball) Ojibwa players sent a ball over the wall of the British stockade and then all of them went inside to retrieve it. Once they had gained access to the fort, they began killing settlers and taking prisoners. By the middle of June, the Senecas had also joined in the rebellion. First they attacked Fort Venango and left no survivors. A day or so later they attacked Fort Le Boeuf, but the British were able to escape before the fort was destroyed. The Senecas then joined forces with the Ottawas, Ojibwas, and Wyandots and carried out a successful siege, which led to the British surrender of Fort Presque Isle on June 20.

Warriors undermine cause

In a little more than a month, nine British forts had been seized and one had been deserted. However, the Detroit post and Fort Pitt in Pennsylvania remained intact. During the standoff at Detroit, the British troops managed to repulse Pontiac's combined force of about nine hundred warriors by bringing reinforcements down the Niagara River. Pontiac also fortified his own forces so that the siege gradually turned into a stalemate. In the meantime, at Amherst's suggestion, British soldiers at Fort Pitt used a crude form of biological warfare to hold off a Native American siege. The British secretly circulated smallpox-infected blankets and handkerchiefs among the warriors, producing an epidemic among the Native Americans in the Ohio towns of Delaware, Mingo, and Shawnee.(Smallpox is a contagious, often fatal disease that produces skin sores and high fever. Smallpox was one of numerous diseases brought to North America by Europeans.) The epidemic lasted until the following spring.

In the early weeks of Pontiac's war the Native American allies had gained an advantage over the British, but obstacles to future success became obvious. Many tribal leaders were critical of the acts of torture and cannibalism (eating of human flesh by a human being) committed by warriors during drunken celebration parties at the Ottawa camp near Detroit. Kinochameg, son of the Ojibwa leader Minevavana, traveled from northern Michigan to deliver a speech denouncing the terrible treatment of British prisoners. Representatives of the Delaware and Shawnee tribes also called a council meeting to warn that the war was damaging fur trade with the French. Furthermore, the military confrontations were generating violence and brutality beyond the battlefield. For instance, isolated Native American raids on settlements along the frontier from New York to Maryland had provoked counterattacks from colonists.

Hostilities wane

Throughout the war Pontiac had remained confident that the French would ultimately come to the aid of the tribal alliance. He was not aware, however, that England and France had already signed a peace treaty in London, England, the previous February. When Pontiac learned the French were no longer a possible ally he lost hope that the Native Americans could win the war. In addition, with the approach of winter, his warriors were becoming increasingly anxious about having adequate food and shelter for their families. Then, on October 20, 1763, Pontiac received a letter from Major de Villiers, commander of the French Fort de Chartres on the Mississippi River, advising him to end his campaign. The next day Pontiac called a halt to the siege of Detroit and retreated to the west. Throughout the next year he sustained his opposition to the British, but he was unable to provide effective leadership or direction. The tribal alliances gradually broke up and, apart from scattered Native American raids and attacks, the hostilities came to an end.

Signs peace treaty

In 1765, at a site along the Wabash River in present-day Indiana, Pontiac finally agreed to a preliminary peace pact with the British. He then earned the admiration and respect of the British by subduing rebellious warriors. Pontiac consequently upset many of his Native American followers not only by failing to win the war but also by appearing to cooperate with the enemy. The next year, when Pontiac signed a formal peace treaty at Oswego, he was pardoned by the British for his involvement in the revolt. Yet the chief remained the target of hostile Native Americans. In April 1769, as Pontiac was en route to a trading post at Cahokia, Illinois, he was stabbed to death by Black Dog, a member of the Illinois tribe. Historians speculate that Black Dog may have been paid by British officers who continued to regard Pontiac as a threat. Other accounts indicate that the assassination was arranged in a Native American council and Black Dog was chosen to carry out the task. Pontiac's exact burial site has never been determined.

For further research

Dockstader, Frederick J. *Great North American Indians.* New York: Van Nostrand Reinhold, 1977, pp. 35, 217–19.

Eckert, Allan W. *The Conquerors.* Boston: Little, Brown, 1970.

Waldman, Carl. *Who Was Who in Native American History.* New York: Facts on File, 1990, pp. 279–80.

Popé
c.1625
San Juan Pueblo, New Mexico
c.1690
San Juan Pueblo, New Mexico

Tewa Pueblo medicine man and political leader

Popé was a seventeenth-century revolutionary leader of the Pueblos, a Native American group in present-day New Mexico. Defying laws established by Spanish conquistadors (conquerors), Popé practiced the traditional Pueblo religion and urged Native Americans to reject Roman Catholicism. (Roman Catholicism is a branch of Christianity that is based in Rome, Italy, and headed by the pope.) Popé also advocated a return to the old Pueblo way of life that had existed before the arrival of the Spaniards. In 1680 Popé organized a revolt at Santa Fe against Spanish forces. During the siege four hundred missionaries and colonists were killed, and the Pueblos forced the survivors to flee hundreds of miles southward. The Pueblos were finally rid of the Spanish. Popé then set about removing all traces of Spanish influence: he outlawed the Spanish language, destroyed Catholic churches, and "cleansed" the people who had been baptized by missionaries. Within a decade, however, Popé's power was weakened by Apache raids, internal Pueblo dissension, and his own tyrannical (being abusive with power) rule. In 1692, less than two years after Popé's death, the Spaniards once again conquered the Pueblos.

Spanish conquest of Pueblos

In 1680 Popé organized a revolt that expelled the Spanish from New Mexico, thus ending eighty-two years of oppression that had virtually obliterated the Pueblo way of life. When the conquistadors under **Francisco Vásquez de Coronado** (see entry) passed through Pueblo territory between 1540 and 1542, they forced the Pueblo people from their homes. They were primarily interested in the possibility of finding gold on the land. In 1591 Don Juan de Oñate, the head of a wealthy Spanish family, established his capital at the town he called San Juan. He then ordered Native Americans to move to nearby villages. As friars (clergymen) tried to convert the Native Americans, troops searched for treasure. These actions provoked a rebellion at the Pueblo town of Acoma, where villagers threw the Spaniards over the sides of cliffs. Spanish reinforcements arrived, and in the subsequent fighting more than one thousand native warriors died. Others were tried and convicted, and their hands and feet were chopped off as punishment. Acoma women were enslaved.

After founding the capital of Santa Fe, Spanish officials demanded that Native Americans pay annual taxes in the form agricultural products or other goods in addition to providing forced labor. Some Pueblo people accepted Christianity, although traditionalists continued to resist Spanish efforts to convert them. By the 1770s droughts had begun to reduce the food supply for the growing population, and starving Apaches attacked Pueblo peoples for food. Some Native Americans feared that their old gods had been offended. In 1675 a medicine man named Popé emerged in San Juan and rallied the Pueblos against the Spanish, whom he blamed for the recent hardships and injustices.

Defies Spanish authorities

Little is known about Popé prior to 1675 (a few historians place the date around 1660), other than he had been practicing for some time as a Tewa medicine man (a priestly healer) of the San Juan Pueblo. Around 1675 he became well known for his attempts to prevent Native Americans from following the teachings of Spanish Catholic missionaries. Traveling from village to village, Popé conducted traditional Pueblo ceremonies in kivas (secret chambers) where kachinas (dancers costumed as ancestral spirits) appeared to participants. As punishment for Popé's observance of the Native American religion, the Spanish seized and enslaved his older brother. Shortly thereafter a series of droughts reduced the food supply. Starving Apaches attacked Pueblo peoples, who feared that their gods had been offended by their passive acceptance of Spanish customs and religion.

Popé announced that the droughts were caused by the Spanish friars and demanded that they leave so that rainfall would begin again. As Popé's following increased, Spanish attempts to suppress him caused a panic. In an attempt to impose order, Spanish authorities imprisoned Popé and forty-six other Native American medicine men in Santa Fe. All were charged with witchcraft (use of supernatural powers to influence events) and three were hanged. At this point the Pueblos were frantic, convinced they would die without medicine men to protect them against evil forces. Seventy Native Americans confronted the Spanish governor at Santa Fe and threatened to kill every Spaniard in New Mexico if the medicine men were not released. Finally the governor gave in and freed the prisoners. This show of weakness on the part of the Spanish only further inflamed the Native Americans.

Heads violent revolt

Soon Popé was plotting an organized rebellion. Again he traveled around New Mexico, urging chiefs and medicine men to rid the land of Spaniards and restore traditional Pueblo customs. He dramatized the anger of the gods by staging kachina dances in kivas. Although Popé had substantial support, he knew many Native Americans remained loyal to the Spaniards. Therefore he decreed that any informers would be put to death. To show that he would keep his word he had his brother-in-law executed for spying for the Spanish. By 1680 Popé had formed a tribal alliance and set August 11 as the date for a general revolt. To guard against news of the plan reaching the Spanish, he sent a signal to his most trusted allies—cords that had been tied into knots representing the number of days remaining until August 11. To less trustworthy followers Popé sent cords with knots indicating that August 13 was the day of the planned rebellion. Predictably, the Spanish heard about the August 13 date, but by then the Pueblos had already launched their assault.

Eyewitness account of Pueblo revolt

The Spaniards were so shocked by the Pueblo revolt of 1680 that they collected testimony from Native Americans about the reasons for the rebellion. Excerpted below is the eyewitness account of Don Pedro Nanboa, an elderly Alameda Pueblo who had observed Native resistance to the Spanish for several years. Nanboa's story was recorded through a translator by Spanish official Antonio de Otertmín.

. . . Having been asked his name and of what place he is a native, his condition, and age, he said that his name is Don Pedro Nanboa, that he is a native of the pueblo of Alameda, a widower, and somewhat more than eighty years of age. Asked for what reason the Indians of this kingdom have rebelled, forsaking their obedience to his Majesty and failing in their obligation as Christians, he said that for a long time, because the Spaniards punished sorcerers and idolaters, the nations of the Teguas, Taos, Pecurfes, Pecos, and Jemez had been plotting to rebel and kill the Spaniards and the religious, and that they had been planning constantly to carry it out, down to the present occasion. . . . that what he has heard is that the Indians do not want religious or Spaniards. Because he is so old,

he was in the cornfield when he learned from the Indian rebels who came from the sierra that they had killed the Spaniards of the jurisdiction and robbed all their haciendas [homes], sacking their houses. Asked whether he knows about the Spaniards and religious who were gathered in the pueblo of La Isleta, he said. . . . that they set out to leave the kingdom with those of the said pueblo of La Isleta and the Spaniards—not one of whom remained—taking along their property. The Indians did not fight with them because all the men had gone with the other nations to fight at the villa and destroy the governor and captain-general and all the people who were with him. He declared that the resentment which all the Indians have in their hearts has been so strong, from the time this kingdom was discovered, [by the Spanish] because the religious and the Spaniards took away their idols and forbade their sorceries and idolatries; that they have inherited successively from their old men the things pertaining to their ancient customs; and that he has heard this resentment spoken of since he was of an age to understand. . . .

Antonio de Otertmín

Reprinted in: Kupperman, Karen Ordahl, ed. *Major Problems in American Colonial History. Lexington, Mass.: D. C. Heath and Company, 1993, p. 46.*

Erases Spanish influence

The coordinated attacks were highly successful. Within a few days, the entire Spanish community had retreated to Santa Fe. After several days of fierce fighting the Pueblos burned Santa Fe to the ground. They killed four hundred settlers and forced the survivors to flee southward hundreds of miles to El Paso (a present-day city in Texas). New

Mexico was now totally under control of the Pueblos. Popé ordered that every trace of the Spanish culture be erased. He banned the Spanish language and the Christian religion, and he required converts to be ritually cleansed of their sins with yucca (a plant with long fibrous leaves on a woody base and large white blossoms) suds. Within a short time all evidence of the Spanish presence had vanished. Nevertheless Popé eventually lost the support of his followers, who had become accustomed to European trade goods. More significantly, he was an unwise and unjust ruler, resorting to abuses of power and becoming as brutal as the conquistadors. In addition, the Pueblos were attacked by Apaches, who seized their horses and brought them into contact with other Native cultures. After Popé died sometime around 1690, Pueblo unity eroded. In 1692 the Spanish returned in force and reasserted their authority in the Southwest.

For further research

Biographical Dictionary of Indians of the Americas. Newport Beach, Calif: American Indian Publishers, 1991, pp. 560–61.

Kupperman, Karen Ordahl, ed. *Major Problems in American Colonial History.* Lexington, Mass.: D. C. Heath and Company, 1993, p. 46.

"Popé." http://www.pbs.org/weta/thewest/wpages/wpgs400/w4pope.htm Available July 13, 1999.

Sando, Joe S. *Pueblo Profiles: Cultural Identity through Centuries of Change.* Santa Fe: Clear Light, 1995.

Powhatan

c. 1548
Powhatan (present-day Richmond, Virginia)
1618
Powhatan

Powhatan-Renapé leader

" . . . Why should you destroy us, who have provided you with food? What can you get by war? . . . "

Powhatan.

Portrait: Powhatan.
Reproduced by permission of The Library of Congress.

Powhatan was a major leader of the Powhatans, Renapé-speaking people of the region that is now Virginia. (Powhatan had taken the name of his tribe to signify his power.) Before the arrival of the English he had several other names, including Wahunsonacock ("He Makes an Offering by Crushing with a Falling Weight" or "He Knows How to Crush Them"). He was the main political leader in the area at the time the English were trying to establish their first permanent settlements, most notably Jamestown. Although Powhatan was suspicious of the English, he maintained generally peaceful relations with them. He used his diplomatic skills to avoid confrontation and to stay one step ahead of the colonists' efforts to take power and land from Native Americans. He was a successful politician with other Native American groups as well, forming a confederacy of more than thirty groups that lasted for several years. The peace established by Powhatan lasted until a few years after his death, when his brother Opechancanough led the Powhatans in uprisings against English settlers.

Heads powerful alliance

Powhatan was born around 1548 in a village called Powhatan, which is today the site of Richmond, Virginia. By the late 1500s he presided over the Powhatan Confederacy, an alliance of Native American tribes and villages stretching from the Potomac River to the Tidewater region of Virginia (low-lying land along the Atlantic coast). From his father, Powhatan inherited a confederacy of six tribes, but the ambitious leader quickly expanded his domain. Estimates of the size of the Powhatan Confederacy range from 128 to 200 villages consisting of approximately 9,000 inhabitants and encompassing nearly 30 tribes. In 1612 Powhatan's family reportedly numbered twenty sons and ten daughters (one of whom was **Pocahontas**; see entry), and he was said to have had twelve or more wives.

Communities under Powhatan's rule received military protection and adhered to the confederacy's well-organized system of hunting and trading boundaries. In return, subjects paid a tax to Powhatan in the form of food, pelts (animal skins), copper, and pearls. Europeans who visited Powhatan in the 1600s have described a large structure filled with "treasures," which was probably the chieftain's storehouse and revenue collection center. Around 1608 **John Smith** (see entry), the leader of the Jamestown Colony, described Powhatan as a "tall well-proportioned man . . . his head somewhat gray. . . . His age is near 60; of a very able and hardy body to endure any labor." Others who knew the chieftain described him in the same way. One colonist said he was regal and majestic: "No king, but a kingly figure."

Distrusts Europeans

The society of the Powhatans was greatly influenced by Spanish attempts to set up a mission in the area in 1570 and by English efforts to colonize the Roanoke region in the 1580s. The Europeans introduced new diseases, which greatly reduced the Powhatan population. In the early 1600s English sea captains conducted raids along the Atlantic coast, carrying off many Native Americans as slaves. When the Jamestown expedition landed on the shore of Powhatan's domain in 1607, the English were unaware that they were trespassing on a land ruled by a shrewd and well-organized head of state.

Native American chief Powhatan was crowned king by the English colonists in an effort to establish peace with the Powhatan Confederacy. *Reproduced by permission of Archive Photos, Inc.*

Powhatan could easily have demolished the struggling community, but instead chose to tolerate the English for a time—probably out of a desire to develop trade relations. Despite his interest in acquiring European-made metal tools and weaponry, Powhatan was suspicious of the English colonists. The independent Powhatan villages at the mouth of the Chesapeake Bay shared his distrust of Europeans, and attacked the settlers when they came ashore.

Helps Jamestown colonists

During the early 1600s Powhatan usually resided at Werawocomoco ("Good House"), located on the north side of the lower Pamunkey (York) River. Reportedly, he also had large houses in each of the "kingdoms" he had inherited as well as the "treasure" house on the upper Chickahominy River. Smith was made prisoner there in late 1607 or early 1608 either for coming too close to the treasure house or for other offensive

Powhatan addresses John Smith

In 1609 Powhatan delivered the following speech to John Smith, encouraging the Jamestown colonists to disarm themselves.

I am now grown old, and must soon die; and the succession must descend, in order, to my brothers, Opitchapan, Opekankanough, and Catataugh, and then to my two sisters, and their two daughters. I wish their experience was equal to mine; and that your love to us might not be less than ours to you. Why should you take by force that from us which you can have by love? Why should you destroy us, who have provided you with food? What can you get by war? We can hide our provisions, and fly into the woods; and then you must consequently famish by wronging your friends. What is the cause of your jealousy? You see us unarmed, and willing to supply your wants, if you will come in a friendly manner, and not with swords and guns, as to invade an enemy. I am not so simple, as not to know it is better to eat good meat, lie well, and sleep quietly with my women and children; to laugh and be merry with the English; and, being their friend, to have copper, hatchets, and whatever else I want, than to fly from all, to lie cold in the woods, feed upon acorns, roots, and such trash, and to be so hunted, that I cannot rest, eat, or sleep. In such circumstances, my men must watch, and if a twig should but break, all would cry out, "Here comes Capt. Smith"; and so, in this miserable manner, to end my miserable life; and, Capt. Smith, this might be soon your fate too, through your rashness and unadvisedness. I, therefore, exhort [urge] you to peaceable councils; and, above all, I insist that the guns and swords, the cause of all our jealousy and uneasiness, be removed and sent away.

Reprinted in: Elliott, Emory, and others, eds. **American Literature: A Prentice Hall Anthology.** *Englewood Cliff, New Jersey: Prentice Hall, 1991, pp. 58–59.*

actions. Smith was threatened with execution. According to his own story and various legends, however, he was rescued by Pocahontas, who later persuaded Powhatan to send food to the starving colonists. By most accounts, the Jamestown settlers would have perished had it not been for the assistance of Powhatan.

English writers depicted Powhatan as a very powerful man. They were impressed by the guards who surrounded him and his home. Certainly Powhatan received tribute from many groups but several others were only weakly attached to his confederacy. Many tribes on the north side of the Powhatan River had at least some degree of self-rule. Farther north, Powhatan's control seems to have ended at the Mattaponi River. The English may have wished to portray Powhatan as being more powerful than he actually was because they wanted to control the region. This would be easier to do if all the power belonged to one person. They hoped to make Powhatan a subject of the James I, king of England, thus bringing his territory under British rule. Since it was crucial to gain Powhatan's loyalty, colonial leaders made every effort to befriend him. For instance, in 1609 he was offered a crown from James I. Powhatan reluctantly agreed to have it placed on his head, and in return he sent the king his old moccasins and a cloak.

Remains wary of colonists

In 1614 Pocahontas was captured by the English and converted to Christianity. In 1614 she married **John Rolfe** (see entry), a Jamestown colonist who was credited with starting the tobacco industry in Virginia. In the meantime Powhatan began to turn against the English. He quietly prepared his people for a war that would expel the invaders. His strategy included sending several of his advisors to England to estimate the strength and intentions of the British Empire. One such observer was Uttamatamakin (Tomocomo), who went to England with Pocahontas in 1616. In arguments with officials at the court of James I, Uttamatamakin became known as a vigorous defender of Renapé religion and values. Pocahontas died suddenly in 1617 as she was returning to Virginia from England. Powhatan died the following year. It was left to his brother Opechancanough, in 1622, to wage the war of liberation that had been envisioned by Powhatan. Three hundred colonists were killed, thus setting in motion the English policy of deliberate extermination of Native Americans.

For further research

"Chief Powhatan." http://www.apva.org/ngex/chief.htm Available July 13, 1999.

Elliott, Emory, and others, eds. *American Literature: A Prentice Hall Anthology.* Englewood Cliff, N.J.: Prentice Hall, 1991, pp. 58–59.

Feest, Christian F. *The Powhatan Tribes.* New York: Chelsea House, 1989.

McDaniel, Melissa. *The Powhatan Indians.* New York: Chelsea House, 1995.

Rountree, Helen C. *The Powhatan Indians of Virginia: Their Traditional Culture.* Norman, Okla.: University of Oklahoma Press, 1989.

John Rolfe

May 1585
Norfolk, England
March 22, 1622
Jamestown, Virginia

Virginia colonist, tobacco planter

John Rolfe is perhaps best known today as the Jamestown colonist who married **Pocahontas** (see entry), the Powhatan "princess," in order to seal an alliance between English settlers and the Powhatan tribe. Yet Rolfe had an even greater impact on Virginia. In 1612, two years after he arrived in the colony, he perfected a strain of tobacco for export to England. (Tobacco is a broad-leaf plant that is grown in warm climates. In the seventeenth century it was harvested, dried, and shredded for use in smoking in pipes. Native Americans had long been using tobacco in this manner. Today tobacco is also rolled in small, thin pieces of paper to make cigarettes.) Soon tobacco became a staple Virginia product as well as the first profitable crop to be grown on the mainland of North America. Rolfe's success resulted in a booming export business and laid the foundation for the trading policies of the British Crown (monarchy) in America. His experiments with tobacco crops also brought about profound economic and social changes that affected both the Virginia colonists and their Powhatan neighbors.

" . . . as pleasant, sweet, and strong . . . as any under the sunne."

John Rolfe.

Portrait: John Rolfe.
Reproduced by permission of The Granger Collection Ltd.

283

The cultivation of tobacco in seventeenth-century Virginia. Rolfe's perfecting of tobacco made it one of the New World's most marketable crops.

Reproduced by permission of The Granger Collection Ltd.

Perfects tobacco strain

John Rolfe was born in May 1585, in Norfolk, England, the son of John and Dorothea (Mason) Rolfe. He had a twin brother, Eustacius, who died in childhood. Little is known about Rolfe's life in England, except that he married in 1608. The following year he and his wife sailed for Virginia, and during the voyage their ship wrecked in the Bermuda islands in the West Indies. While in the Bermudas, Rolfe's wife gave birth to a daughter who died in infancy. Tragically, Rolfe's wife died shortly after the couple arrived in Virginia, in 1610. Not long after his arrival Rolfe realized that the colony was in trouble. The problems had begun at the outset, when the Virginia Company, led by **John Smith** (see entry) and others, first came ashore in 1607. Most members of the group were English gentlemen who sought quick wealth in Virginia. Moreover, they were all single—no women came with the earliest colonists—and they were unaccustomed to working for a living. Within a year, poor planning and lack of discipline led to the deaths of

67 of the original 105 settlers. The high mortality (death) rate continued (400 out of 500 men were dead by 1609), which meant further instability in the colony.

Upon his arrival, Rolfe was intent on finding a crop that would assure economic security and profit. He decided to try cultivating tobacco because he believed that it could be exported to England, but first he had to grow it. He first experimented with a type of plant then being grown by Native Americans. Most Englishmen found the tobacco to be too harsh when smoked, however, so Rolfe imported seeds from the West Indies. Finally he developed a tobacco leaf that was "as pleasant, sweet, and strong . . . as any under the sunne." Rolfe's new strain thrived in Virginia soil and the colonists set about planting their crop. They exported the tobacco to eager buyers in England, becoming the first Europeans to produce a marketable crop on the mainland of North America. The English king, James I, initially threatened to outlaw tobacco, calling it a "stinking weed." Yet demand was strong and the market flourished. Eventually tobacco sales yielded so much tax money for England that James relented and came to rely on the income.

Trade brings change

With trade booming and tobacco fetching high prices, prosperous Chesapeake farmers planted primarily tobacco and imported (brought from another country) all other necessities except food and timber. Exporting (sending to another country) tobacco became so profitable that colonists even planted it in the streets of Jamestown. Dependence on a single crop resulted in a plantation economy that continued throughout the colonial period. It also changed the labor situation in Virginia. Even before the tobacco boom the Virginia Company had sent over indentured servants. (Indentured servants were laborers who usually worked four to seven years in exchange for free passage to Virginia and room and board. At the end of their service they often received a small plot of land.) Thriving trade brought about an increased need for labor. Since cultivating tobacco also required huge tracts of tillable soil, the colonists expanded outward into small settlements along the James River. As they encroached (to advance beyond the usual or proper limits) farther onto the land of the Powhatan tribe,

The tobacco industry in Virginia

John Rolfe developed a strain of tobacco that thrived in Virginia soil. The Jamestown colony exported the tobacco to England, and trade was soon booming. Because tobacco fetched a high price, Chesapeake growers planted primarily tobacco and imported all other necessities except food and timber. In 1616 the colony exported 2,300 pounds of tobacco to England. Three years later the total had risen to 20,000 pounds, and by 1626 Virginia was shipping 260,000 pounds abroad. But the boom ended in 1629. During the 1630s the price of tobacco fell from sixteen to five pennies per pound. Yet by 1700 planters were exporting 38 million pounds of tobacco. During the eighteenth century, tobacco exports fluctuated between 25 million and 160 million pounds. Although exporting the crop remained profitable, it would never again command the exorbitant prices of the first quarter of the seventeenth century. To maintain their profits, planters needed to grow and export more tobacco, but the crop depleted the soil. Therefore Chesapeake planters found their yield declined after only three or four years. That problem resulted in planters either moving inland—thus taking more Native American land—or switching to planting wheat.

the growing English population put additional pressure on the Native Americans.

Pocahontas

Because of his economic success, Rolfe was a prominent colonist when he met Pocahontas in 1612. She was a young daughter of **Powhatan** (see entry), principal chief of the Powhatans, who headed an alliance of more than thirty tribes in the region. (Powhatan took the name of his tribe to signify his power.) Powhatan welcomed the Jamestown colonists in 1607 and maintained friendly relations with them. He and Pocahontas had even saved the Englishmen from starvation during their first winter in Virginia by providing them with food. In 1608, two years before Rolfe's arrival at Jamestown, twelve-year-old Pocahontas had supposedly saved Smith from being executed by Powhatan, who had realized that the colonists were not interested in maintaining peace with the Native Americans. The following year Smith returned to England and Pocahontas never visited the colony again. In the meantime, Powhatan had decided to prohibit trade between the Powhatans and the settlers. He also began conducting guerilla warfare (a form of unplanned, or unconventional, warfare that involves surprise attacks) and taking Englishmen hostage.

In early 1612 Samuel Argall, who had taken over Smith's position in Jamestown, learned that Pocahontas was living with the neighboring Patawamake tribe. Since the colonists were still suffering from Powhatan's trading sanctions (prohibiting trade), Argall decided to take Pocahontas captive in order to force Powhatan to release English hostages. Coaxing her on board his ship, he sailed off with her to Jamestown. The Englishmen announced that they were holding Pocahontas, yet their negotiations with the Powhatans did not go well. Powhatan was willing to turn over the English hostages, but he would not give up weapons and tools that he claimed were stolen from him. Shortly thereafter the Powhatans attacked the colonists. Argall and acting Jamestown governor Thomas Dale brought Pocahontas to help conduct negotiations. She refused to meet with her father's representatives, choosing instead to remain with the English. According to a letter by Dale quoted in *Purchas his Pilgrimes,* Pocahontas claimed that "if her father had loved her, he would not value her lesse then old Swords, Peeces [guns], or Axes: wherefore shee should still dwell with the English men, who loved her."

Marries Pocahontas

At this point Rolfe entered the picture. He had met Pocahontas while she was in the care of the Reverend Alexander Whitaker at Henrico, a new community near Jamestown. Whitaker presided at Pocahontas's baptism when she took the name "Rebecca" as a sign of her conversion to Christianity. Carefully considering the situation, Rolfe decided he would marry Pocahontas for political reasons. In a letter to Dale he outlined his plan, which he said was "for the good of the Plantacon, the honor of or Countrye, for the glorye of God, for myne owne salvacon." After receiving the blessing of both Powhatan and Dale, Pocahontas and Rolfe were married at Jamestown in April

The marriage of John Rolfe and Pocahontas.

Reproduced by permission of Corbis-Bettmann.

1614. Thus began the "Peace of Pocahontas," a long period of friendship between the English and Powhatan tribes.

Returns to England

In 1615 Pocahontas bore Rolfe a son named Thomas. At the invitation of the Virginia Company, which was grateful for renewed trade relations with the Powhatans, the Rolfes went to England in 1616. Although English society was at first reluctant to accept Rolfe's marriage to a Native American, Pocahontas was soon the talk of the town. She was admitted into the presence of Queen Anne and later received by King James I. Rolfe did not share in the honor, however, partly because the king was upset with Rolfe for marrying a foreign princess without his permission. James also did not approve of Rolfe's association with tobacco.

By 1617 Pocahontas's health had begun to fail. Rolfe took her to the village of Brentford outside London, then arranged to leave for Virginia in mid-March. Pocahontas was critically ill, however, and she died within days. Rolfe returned to Virginia, where he was married for a third time, to Jane Pierce. In 1622 the Powhatans launched a full-fledged massacre of the English, killing about a quarter of the Jamestown population. Rolfe died in the fighting.

For further research

Stephen, Leslie, and Sidney Lee, eds. *The Dictionary of National Biography.* London, England: Oxford University Press, 1917, pp. 157–58.

Mary White Rowlandson

1635 (or 1637)
Somersetshire, England
1711?
Wethersfield, Connecticut

Writer of a famous captivity narrative

Mary White Rowlandson, the wife of a Puritan clergyman, lived with her family on the New England frontier during the late seventeenth century. The violent events of King Philip's War (1675–76; see **Metacom** entry) transformed Rowlandson from a typical Puritan woman to a best-selling author. On a night in February 1676, a Wampanoag raiding party abducted Rowlandson, her three children, and several other colonists. One of her children died in captivity. Three months later Rowlandson and her two surviving children were released when her husband paid a ransom to the Wampanoags. She wrote about this experience in *The Narrative of the Captivity and Restauration of Mrs. Mary Rowlandson* (a shortened title), which she originally composed for her children. *The Narrative* was published in 1682 to resounding success. Rowlandson's account is important to historians because it provides a realistic description of life on the American frontier and depicts the deep Christian faith of a Puritan woman. On another level, it also portrays the futile efforts of Native Americans to prevent colonists from taking over their land.

Settles on frontier

Mary White Rowlandson was born in Somersetshire, England, around 1635 (some sources report 1637), one of nine children of John and Joane (West) White. During her early childhood the Whites emigrated (moved from one country to another) to America and settled at Salem, a town in the Puritan colony of Massachusetts. (The Puritans were a Christian religious group who preached strict moral and spiritual codes.) In 1653 the family moved to Lancaster, Massachusetts, a new village on the frontier, about thirty miles west of Boston. In 1656 Mary White married Joseph Rowlandson, a Puritan parson (clergyman) and the first permanent minister in Lancaster. The couple made their home on a hill overlooking Ropers Brook (a commemorative plaque now marks the site). For the next twenty years Mary Rowlandson led the life of a typical mother and parson's wife. From 1657 to 1669 she gave birth to four children, one of whom died in infancy. Then, in early 1676, Rowlandson was snatched and thrust into a permanent place in early American history.

Hostilities intensify

A few years after the Rowlandsons were married, hostilities intensified between the Puritans and local Native American tribes. Tensions had been building since the death, in 1661, of the Wampanoag leader **Massasoit** (see entry), an ally of the Puritans. Massasoit's son and successor, **Metacom** (called King Philip; see entry), maintained control of Wampanoag territory. Yet he became alarmed when the Puritans began taking more and more Native American land. Metacom feared the survival of his people was being threatened. War broke out in January 1775 when Puritan authorities in the town of Plymouth executed three Wampanoag warriors on the charge of murdering an Englishman. The conflict raged for eighteen months, mainly in towns on the border between the Massachusetts colony and Native American territory.

Lancaster raided

Residents of Lancaster anticipated an attack, so Joseph Rowlandson went to Boston to obtain military aid. At dawn on February 10, 1676, while Rowlandson was away, a party of four

Native Americans attacking a colonial settlement, a scene similar to the one Mary Rowlandson describes in her narrative.
Reproduced by permission of The Granger Collection.

hundred Native Americans raided Lancaster. Burning houses and killing settlers, they attacked the Rowlandson home, where Mary, her three children, and thirty-two villagers were hiding. The warriors killed twelve people, including Rowlandson's sister. They captured the surviving colonists, among whom were Rowlandson and her children. When Joseph Rowlandson returned to Lancaster he found that his house had burned to the ground and his family had disappeared. Later, in

The Narrative, Mary Rowlandson recalled how she felt when she was being taken hostage: "I had often before this said, that if the Indians should come, I should chuse rather to be killed by them then taken alive but when it came to the tryal my mind changed; their glittering weapons so daunted my spirit, that I chose rather to go along with those (as I may say) ravenous Bears, then that moment to end my dayes."

Rowlandson a prisoner and slave

In the dead of winter the warriors took the captives westward into Native American territory, subjecting them to cruel treatment along the way. During the siege Mary Rowlandson and her six-year-old daughter Sarah had been wounded from gunshots. Her older children, Joseph Jr. and Mary, were apparently unharmed. On the trip through the wilderness Sarah was deprived of food and water. She died nine days later. Rowlandson was then separated from the two older children and sent to live as a slave with sagamore (secondary chief) Quanopin, brother-in-law of Metacom, and his wife Wetamoo.

Rowlandson was in captivity for nearly twelve weeks. During this time she helped the Native Americans as they foraged (to wander in search of provisions) for food and hunted game (wild animals) in the New England region. Traveling to the Connecticut River and into New Hampshire, they then returned to the Lancaster area. In *The Narrative* Rowlandson described twenty "removes," or separate campsites, that the Native Americans set up on their journey. Because her wounds were soon healed with oak leaves, she usually walked and carried heavy loads. She learned to tolerate Native American food such as nuts, grain meal, horsemeat, and game. Rowlandson described sleeping on the frozen ground and being sick, lonely, and frightened. A continuing theme in *The Narrative* is the possibility of violence and death that threatened both Rowlandson and the Native Americans daily. At first she was not treated well by her captors, who were frequently hungry and miserable themselves. Eventually, however, she won them over with her sewing and knitting skills. Wetamoo in particular was charitable toward her. Rowlandson was allowed to see her two children on occasion, but they remained separated from her.

Hannah Duston scalps captors

Hannah Duston (1657–1736) was another frontier woman taken captive by Native Americans. She was living near Haverhill, Massachusetts, with her husband Thomas, a farmer and bricklayer, when Native American warriors attacked the town on March 15, 1697. Hannah had recently given birth to her twelfth child, and that day a neighbor, Mary Neff, was helping out during her recovery. Thomas witnessed the raid while he was working in the field. As the war party approached the farm, he took his eleven older children to a safe hiding place. However, he could not rescue Hannah, Neff, and his infant son. The three captives were taken north toward Canada by twenty Native Americans, and during the march the warriors killed the baby. Eventually they stopped at a Native American settlement on an island off the coast of New Hampshire. There Duston and Neff met Samuel Lennardson, an Englishman who was also a captive. When the three prisoners were told that harsh punishment was in store for them, they decided to fight for their lives. During the night of March 30, Duston and Lennardson attacked their sleeping captors with hatchets. Lennardson killed one Native American and Duston killed nine others. As Duston, Lennardson, and Neff started to run away they realized the settlers at Haverhill might not believe their story. So they went back and scalped their victims. After they returned to Haverhill they took the scalps to the General Court in Boston as evidence of their daring feat. Duston received a cash reward, then returned to Haverhill to live quietly with her husband. Later the Dustons had their thirteenth and last child.

Sustained by faith

Rowlandson was sustained throughout the ordeal by her Christian faith. She found great comfort in a Bible that was given to her by a Wampanoag warrior, who had stolen it during a raid. She met Metacom, leader of King Philip's War, several times while she was in captivity. In early March, Metacom summoned Rowlandson to his "General Court" to discuss selling her back to her husband. Once they had agreed upon a ransom—two coats, half a bushel of seed corn, some tobacco, and twenty pounds (an amount of British money)—a message was sent to Boston. Joseph Rowlandson and several others, including John Hoar, a resident of Concord, engaged in negotiations

From *The Narrative of the Captivity and Restauration of Mrs. Mary Rowlandson:*

On the 10th of February, 1675, came the Indians with great numbers upon Lancaster. Their first coming was about sunrising.

Hearing the noise of some guns, we looked out; several houses were burning, and the smoke ascending to heaven. There were five persons taken in one house; the father and the mother and a suckling child they knocked on the head; the other two they took and carried away alive. There were two others, who, being out of their garrison upon some occasion, were set upon; one was knocked on the head, the other escaped. Another there was who, running along, was shot and wounded, and fell down; he begged of them his life, promising them money (as they told me), but they would not hearken to him, but knocked him in the head, and stripped him naked, and split open his bowels. Another seeing many of the Indians about his barn ventured and went out, but was quickly shot down. There were three others belonging to the same garrison who were killed; the Indians, getting up upon the roof of the barn, had advantage to shoot down upon them over their fortification. Thus these murderous wretches went on burning and destroying before them.

At length they came and beset our own house, and quickly it was the dolefulest [most grievous] day that ever mine eyes saw. The house stood upon the edge of a hill; some of the Indians got behind the hill, others into the barn, and others behind anything that could shelter them; from all which places they shot against the house, so that the bullets seemed to fly like hail, and quickly they wounded one man among us, then another, and then a third. About two hours (according to my observation in that amazing time) they had been about the house before they prevailed to fire it; they fired it once, and one ventured out and quenched it, but they quickly fired it again, and that took. Now is the dreadful hour come that I have often heard of, but now mine eyes see it. Some in our house were fighting for their lives, others wallowing in their blood, the house on fire over our heads, and the bloody heathen [uncivilized or irreligious person] ready to knock us on the head if we stirred out. . . .

Reprinted in: Colbert, David, ed. *Eyewitness to America*. New York: Pantheon Books, 1997, pp. 33–34.

with Metacom. Finally, on May 2, 1676, Hoar arrived unarmed at the Wampanoag camp with the ransom. When Rowlandson was released the Native Americans bid her a fond farewell, evidence that she had established a degree of friendship with her captors. The Rowlandson children were freed from separate locations a few weeks later.

Soon after Rowlandson's release King Philip's War came to an end. In August 1676 the colonists executed Metacom and sold his wife and children into slavery in the West

Indies. The Wampanoag population was devastated during the conflict. Although the settlers suffered six hundred casualties, three thousand Native Americans lost their lives.

Narrative immediate success

The Rowlandsons lived in Boston until April 1677, when Joseph was appointed pastor of the church at Wethersfield, Connecticut. Upon his death in 1678, the town of Wethersfield voted to give Mary Rowlandson a pension of thirty pounds a year for the rest of her life. By 1682 Rowlandson had written *The Narrative,* an account of her experiences in captivity, which she had intended to give her children. The manuscript was published that year in Boston, however, and was an immediate commercial success. The date of Rowlandson's death is not certain, but she is believed to have died in 1711.

In *The Narrative* Rowlandson uses a simple but vivid style to describe the Wampanoag raid on her home and the harrowing ordeal of her captivity. The account is also a testament to Rowlandson's deep religious faith. She cited passages from the Bible at least sixty-five times, and she wrote that her release was evidence of God's goodwill for true Christians. Rowlandson generally depicted the Wampanoags as instruments of the Devil, yet she also revealed their tender, human side. Scholars value the book for Rowlandson's portrayal of the Native Americans, especially Metacom, and for her description of a war that led to the end of Native culture in New England. Since 1682 *The Narrative* has appeared in at least thirty editions and has become a classic of frontier literature.

For further research

Colbert, David, ed. *Eyewitness to America.* New York: Pantheon Books, 1997, pp. 33–34.

Cott, Nancy F., ed. "Hannah Duston." In *The Young Oxford History of Women in the United States: Biographical Supplement and Index.* New York: Oxford University Press, 1995, p. 54.

James, Edward T., and others, eds. *Notable American Women,* Volume III. Cambridge, Mass.: Belknap Press of Harvard University Press, 1971, pp. 200–03.

"Mary White Rowlandson" in *The Puritans: American Literature Colonial Period (1608-1700).* http://www.falcon.jmu.edu/-ramseyil/amicol.htm Available July 13, 1999.

Rowlandson, Mary. *The Narrative of the Captivity and Restauration of Mrs. Mary Rowlandson.* Excerpted in *American Literature: A Prentice Hall Anthology.* Emory Elliott and others, eds. Englewood Cliffs, N.J.: Prentice Hall, 1991, pp. 169–85.

Salisburg, Neal, ed. *Sovereignty and Goodness of God.* Boston: Bedford Books, 1997.

Samuel Sewall

**March 28, 1652
Hampshire, England
January 1, 1730
Boston, Massachusetts**

Massachusetts businessman and judge

"Tis pity there should be more caution used in buying a horse, or a little lifeless dust, than there is in purchasing men and women. . . . "

Samuel Sewall.

Portrait: Samuel Sewall.
Reproduced by permission of Archive Photos, Inc.

Samuel Sewall was a prominent businessman and judge in Boston during a time of social and political upheaval in the Massachusetts colony. He is perhaps best known for making a dramatic public apology for the role he played as a judge in the Salem witch trials, which resulted in the executions of nineteen people. Sewall is also famous for his diary, a remarkable work that spans more than fifty years and provides modern historians with a vivid picture of life in Puritan New England. (The Puritans were a Christian group who observed strict moral and spiritual codes; they controlled social and political life in Massachusetts.) Sewall also was one of the first colonists to speak out against the keeping of African slaves.

Begins long public career

Samuel Sewall was born in Hampshire, England, on March 28, 1652, the son of Henry and Jane (Dummer) Sewall. When he was nine years old, his parents emigrated (moved from one country to another) to Newbury, Massachusetts, where he was educated at a private school. In 1671 he graduated from Harvard College with a bachelor's degree and three years later earned a master's degree from the same institution. Sewall was then ordained a minister, but he left the church to go into business when he married Hannah Hull in 1675. Sewall's father-in-law, John Hull, was the master of the mint (a government agency that prints money) for the Massachusetts Bay Colony and therefore had extensive connections in the business community. At Hull's urging, Sewall moved to Boston in 1681 to take over management of the colony's printing press. By the early 1690s he was a prominent figure in Boston business and political circles. He was a banker, publisher, international trader, and member of the colonial court. Although Sewall had no formal legal training, he also served as a judge (at that time a law degree was not required).

Sewall began his long career as a government official in 1683, when he was appointed to the general court. The following year he was elected to the Massachusetts council (governing body). While visiting England on business in 1684, he became involved in unsuccessful efforts to convince British officials to maintain the Massachusetts Bay Colony charter in its present form. Massachusetts Bay was the only self-governing English colony in America (see **John Winthrop** entry). However, Britain revoked the charter because Massachusetts Bay officials were illegally operating a mint. They were also basing voting rights on religious affiliation instead of property ownership and discriminating against Anglicans (members of the Church of England, the official religion of the country); the majority of the Massachusetts colonists were Puritans.

The Salem witch trials

In 1691 Britain forced the Massachusetts Bay Colony to accept a charter that united it with Plymouth (see **William Bradford** entry) and Maine (see Ferdinando Gorges box in **Thomas Morton** entry) to form the Massachusetts colony. Under the new charter, church membership could no longer be a requirement for voting, although Congregationalism (a branch of Puritanism organized according to independent church congregations) remained the established (official) church. Sewall was named a councilor (advisor) in the new royal government, a position he held until 1725, when he decided not to seek reelection.

The execution of Salem "witches." Although Sewall participated in the trials that led to the executions, he eventually regretted his role in the tragedy.
Reproduced by permission of The Granger Collection Ltd.

Historians note that the loss of the original charter led to widespread anxiety in Massachusetts, which may be one of the main reasons for the infamous witchcraft hysteria that followed. Puritan officials believed the colony was under an evil spell cast by witches (people, usually women, with supernatural powers), who had signed a compact with the Devil, the ultimate evil force. Witches were supposedly seeking revenge on particular members of the community. According to the Puritans, the compact empowered a witch to perform such acts as causing a child's death, making crops fail, preventing cream from being churned into butter, or producing sterility (inability to conceive offspring) in cattle. They also believed witches entered the bodies of animals and became beings called "familiars" who prowled around undetected. Yet the witches could be discovered through other forms of witchcraft. The prominent Puritan leader Increase Mather (see box in **Cotton Mather** entry) wrote *Remarkable Providence,* a handbook on how to identify a witch. He actively supported holding trials to rid the colony of witches.

"the blame and shame of it"

Samuel Sewall regretted his participation as a judge in the Salem witch trials of 1692–93. On January 14, 1697—a special day of atonement set aside by the Massachusetts legislature—Sewall stood and faced the congregation in the Old South Church at Boston. The Reverend Samuel Willard then read aloud this statement Sewall had written:

> Samuel Sewall, sensible of the reiterated [repeated] strokes of God upon himself and his family; and being sensible, that as to the guilt contracted, upon the opening of the late Commission of Oyer and Terminator [the court that conducted the witchcraft trials] at Salem (to which the order for this day relates), he is, upon many accounts, more concerned than any that he knows of, desires to take the blame and shame of it, asking pardon of men, and especially desiring prayers that God, who has an unlimited authority, would pardon that sin and all his other sins; personal and relative: And according to his infinite benignity [kindness], and sovereignty [supreme power], not visit the sin of him, or of any other, upon himself or any of his, nor upon the land: But that He [God] would powerfully defend him against all temptations to sin, for the future; and vouchsafe him the efficacious [having the power to produce a desired effect], saving conduct of his word and spirit.

Reprinted in: Gunn, Giles, ed. **Early American Writing.** *New York: Penguin Books, 1994, pp. 246–47.*

In June 1692, when the Puritans decided to hold formal witch trials in Salem, Massachusetts governor William Phips appointed Sewall as a special commissioner (judge) on the court. Meeting in July and August, Sewall and the other judges interrogated suspected witches and gave them a chance to reject the validity of their compact with the Devil. A suspected witch was usually falsely accused by other members of the community, and soon widespread accusations paralyzed the area. If the suspects opened themselves to God, they would be reaccepted into the community. But many did not repent. The court ultimately sentenced nineteen people, most of whom were women, to death. The executions were carried out in September: eighteen were hanged and a man was crushed to death. Almost immediately Sewall began to regret the role he played in this tragedy, and the guilt weighed increasingly upon his conscience. In fact, he felt he had greater responsibility in the matter than any of the other judges.

Recants role in trials

By 1697 Massachusetts officials realized that witchcraft hysteria was out of control and that the trials had been a terrible mistake, so the legislature designated January 14 as a special day of atonement (expression of regret and request for forgiveness). Taking this opportunity to make a public confession of his sins, Sewall wrote an admission of error and guilt. Then he stood and faced the congregation in the Old South Church at Boston as the Reverend Samuel Willard read the statement aloud. Sewall was the only judge who publicly admitted his own guilt. Increase Mather and his son Cotton, who were a motivating force behind the witch hunts, eventually were instrumental in bringing the trials to an end. Yet the Mathers expressed their doubts only in published written works.

Opposes slavery

After Sewall made his public apology he continued to be a part of governmental affairs and held various judicial offices. He also became involved in abolitionist (antislavery) efforts. In 1700 he published *The Selling of Joseph,* an essay in which he argued against the keeping of African slaves. Now considered one of the earliest antislavery statements, it is frequently reprinted in American history and literature texts. (Quaker minister **John Woolman** (see entry) is credited with organizing the first successful abolitionist movement, in 1743.) Sewall also advocated that Native Americans be placed on reservations and taught the English language and social customs. Colonial governments had been adopting this policy since the mid-1600s. The reservation system eventually resulted in the total extinction of the Native American way of life by the early nineteenth century.

Writes famous diary

Sewall wrote numerous historical and religious works as well as unpublished poetry during his lifetime. He is best known, however, for his diary, in which he gave a vivid picture of Puritan life in seventeenth- and eighteenth-century New England. (The diary spans the period from 1674 to 1729; there were no entries from 1677 to 1685.) Sewall was married three times. Hannah Sewall, with whom he had fourteen chil-

from *The Selling of Joseph*

Samuel Sewall had long been troubled by the practice of slavery in the American colonies, but he had never acted on his views. Then, while he was serving as a judge in the Massachusetts General Court, he had to make a decision on a petition to free an African couple who were being held in bondage. Sewall therefore resolved to issue a public statement against the holding of African slaves. The result was *The Selling of Joseph* (1700), which is considered one of the earliest expressions of the abolitionist cause. The Joseph in the title is one of the heroes in the Book of Genesis in the Old Testament of the Bible. The favorite son of Jacob and Rachel, Joseph was sold into slavery by his brothers. They were jealous of his ambitions and the coat of many colors that Jacob had given to him.

In the opening of *The Selling of Joseph* Sewall argued that "originally, and naturally, there is no such thing as slavery.

Joseph was rightfully no more a slave to [his brothers] than they were to him; and they had no more authority to sell him than they had to slay him. . . . 'Tis pity there should be more caution used in buying a horse, or a little lifeless dust, than there is in purchasing men and women. . . ." Sewall went on to compare Joseph's situation with that of African slaves: "It is likewise most lamentable to think how, in taking negroes out of Africa and selling of them here, that which God has joined together men do boldly rend asunder; men from their country, husbands from their wives, parents from their children. How horrible is the uncleanness, immorality, if not murder, that the [slave] ships are guilty of that bring great crowds of these miserable men and women [to America]. . . . "

Reprinted in: Gunn, Giles, ed. Early American Writing. *New York: Penguin Books, 1994, pp. 254–57.*

dren, died in 1717. In 1719 he wed Abigail Melyen, who died the following year. One of the most amusing passages in Sewall's diary is his account of courting (seeking to marry) Katherine Winthrop. He wrote that he gave her such gifts as sermons, gingerbread, and sugared almonds. Yet she would not be won over unless he promised to wear a wig and buy a coach. Finally unable to reach a marriage agreement with Winthrop, Sewall turned his affections elsewhere and, at age seventy, took Mary Gibbs as his third wife. He died eight years later, in 1730.

For further research

Elliott, Emory, and others, eds. *American Literature: A Prentice Hall Anthology.* Englewood Cliffs, N.J., 1991, pp. 215–17.

Gunn, Giles, ed. *Early American Writing.* New York: Penguin Books, 1994, pp. 246–47, 254–57.

Images from the Salem Witchcraft Trails. http://www.law.umkc.edu/faculty /projects/ftrials/salem/SA Available July 13, 1999.

Johnson, Allen, and others, eds. *Dictionary of American Biography.* New York: Scribner, 1946–1958, pp. 610–12.

Stephen, Leslie, and Sidney Lee, eds. *The Dictionary of National Biography.* London, England: Oxford University Press, 1917, pp. 1217–18.

Winslow, Ola Elizabeth. *Samuel Sewall of Boston.* New York: Macmillan, 1964.

John Smibert

1688
Edinburgh, Scotland
March 1751

First portrait painter in colonial America

John Smibert (also Smybert) was the first portrait painter to come to America. After settling in Boston (then located in the Massachusetts Colony), he exerted a profound influence on eighteenth-century American art. Smibert's training in the fashionable Dutch-influenced style of portraiture (the making of portraits) brought a new sophistication to painting in New England. Most of the leading citizens of Boston were his clients. Smibert is credited with organizing the first art show in America. He also influenced a number of young American artists.

"Thy Fame, O *Smibert,* shall the Muse rehearse,/And sing her Sister-Art [painting] in softer Verse."

American poet Mather Byles.

Apprenticed as house painter

John Smibert was born in Edinburgh, Scotland, in 1688, where he was raised as a Presbyterian (a Protestant denomination of the Christian religion). While working for seven years as an apprentice to a house painter and plasterer in Edinburgh, he developed an interest in drawing. Upon completing his apprenticeship he moved to London, England. For a time he barely made a living by working for coach painters and copying old pictures for an art dealer. Finally he was admitted to an art academy in London, where he studied with

305

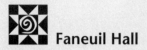

Faneuil Hall

John Smibert, the first portrait painter in America, is credited with having a lasting impact on early American art. He also dabbled in architecture. In 1742 he designed Faneuil Hall, a public market and meeting hall in Boston, Massachusetts. The building was commissioned by the wealthy merchant Peter Faneuil, who gave it to the city. Faneuil Hall burned in 1761 but was later rebuilt. During the American Revolution (1775–83) colonists met there to discuss political and military plans, and the building became known as "the cradle of liberty." Faneuil Hall is still in use today as a market, meeting hall, and museum.

Godfrey Kneller from 1713 until 1716. Kneller's style had influenced several generations of British portrait painters.

Starts career as portrait painter

After his time studying with Kneller, Smibert returned to Edinburgh, where he supported himself for a few years as a professional portrait painter. Finally, when there was no longer a demand for portraits, Smibert left for Italy in 1719. For the next three years he had a successful career painting portraits and copying works from the great art collections in Florence and Rome. He also bought paintings for his own growing collection. Returning to England in 1722, Smibert established a studio in London, where he achieved a modest reputation but no great distinction. His fortunes took a dramatic turn, however, when he met the Irish philosopher and Anglican dean (church official) George Berkeley.

Smibert had joined a society called the "Virtuosi of London." Among the members were artists John Wootton, Thomas Gibson, George Vertue, and Bernard Lens. One of the sitters (people who pose for the painting of their portraits) was Berkeley, who was then dean of Derry, Ireland. Smibert began painting a large group portrait of the "Virtuosi," but he never completed the work. In 1728, however, he did finish a portrait of Berkeley, which now hangs in the National Portrait Gallery in London. That year Smibert also accepted Berkeley's invitation to teach painting, drawing, and architecture at a new college Berkeley hoped to establish in Bermuda (an island in the Caribbean Sea) for planters' children and Native Americans.

Paints *Bermuda Group*

Smibert arrived with Berkeley's party at Newport, Rhode Island, in 1729. The plan was to settle there while Berkeley acquired funding for the college from the British Parliament. During the two-year wait Smibert commemorated the enterprise in his best-known painting, *The Bermuda Group* (also called *Bishop Berkeley and His Entourage*), which contains a self-portrait. The first group portrait painted in America, the work is now owned by Yale University in New Haven, Connecticut. A smaller version hangs in the National Portrait Gallery of Ireland in Dublin. Since the Bermuda project was never approved, Berkeley returned to England. Yet even before his patron (financial supporter) left, Smibert had found his niche in America. Shortly after reaching Newport, he had moved to Boston, where he pursued a lucrative career as a portrait painter.

Becomes first American artist

By 1730, less than a year after arriving in Boston, Smibert had gained wide recognition as a painter. He attracted clients to his studio with his own paintings as well as his copies of the old masters' works and with items from his personal art collection. At that time he reportedly organized the first art show in America. Within eight months he had completed twenty-seven portraits. Among his subjects were merchant Peter Faneuil, who financed the building of the original Faneuil Hall, and judges **Samuel Sewall** (see entry), Nathaniel Byfield, and Edmund Quincy. In 1730 Smibert married Mary Williams, daughter of Nathaniel Williams, the prominent master of the Boston Latin School. The Smiberts had two children. (Their son Nathaniel, who also became a portrait painter, died in 1756.) After five years in Boston, Smibert had painted over one hundred portraits. Although his work would have been considered only average in Britain, American colonists praised the portraits for their lifelike poses, elegant technique, and perceptive interpretation. *The Bermuda Group* hung in Smibert's studio until the end of his life, attracting local admirers as well as travelers from other colonies.

Influences other painters

Smibert's reputation also attracted numerous customers who purchased imported prints and art supplies from a shop he kept along with his studio. Aspiring young Boston painters such as John Greenwood came for support and advice on portraiture. Other American artists incorporated many of Smibert's techniques into their own work, thus extending his influence beyond Boston. Among them were John Singleton Copley, Washington Allston, and John Trumbull. Smibert also dabbled in architecture, designing Faneuil Hall in 1742. As he settled into a prosperous life, however, his portraits became less imaginative. Yet when Smibert died in 1751, he left a lasting impact on American art.

For further research

Foote, Henry W. *John Smibert, Painter.* New York: Da Capo Press, Inc., 1969.

Saunders, Richard H. *John Smibert: Colonial America's First Portrait Painter.* New Haven, Conn.: Yale University Press, 1995.

John Smith

January 6, 1580
Lincolnshire, England
June 1631
London, England

Leader of Jamestown Colony

> "At the minute of my execution, [Pocahontas] . . . hazarded the beating out of her own braines to save mine."
>
> *John Smith.*

John Smith was one of the original seven council members (governors) of Jamestown, Virginia, the first permanent English settlement in America. Smith was a colorful figure as well as an author, whose works about life in early Virginia are still read today. His resourcefulness was invaluable to the Jamestown colonists, who lacked the motivation or skills to survive the harsh circumstances of a strange land. In addition, Smith was one of the few Englishmen to regard Native Americans as fellow human beings. He is perhaps best known for being saved from execution by **Pocahontas** (see entry), daughter of **Powhatan** (see entry), the powerful leader of a large Native American confederacy known as the Powhatan people. Although historians have questioned the truth of this story, it remains one of the most popular legends in American history.

Pursues military career

John Smith was born in Lincolnshire, England, to George and Alice (Rickards) Smith. His father was a farmer who made a comfortable living by working his own farm and leasing another from Peregrine Bertie, Lord Willoughby.

Portrait: John Smith.
Reproduced by permission of The Library of Congress.

309

Unlike a majority of English children at the time, Smith attended grammar school, where he learned to read and write. He also attracted the attention of Lord Willoughby, whose patronage (financial and social support) helped him leave the farms of Lincolnshire, and pursue interests other than farming. When Smith was fifteen he was apprenticed to (learned a trade in exchange for working) a merchant at the seaport of King's Lynn, but soon decided he did not want to work in the mercantile trade. Upon his father's death in 1596 he received a small inheritance. Shortly thereafter he joined the French army.

In late 1596 or early 1597 Smith left England for the Netherlands to participate in a French military campaign against Spain. After a peace treaty was signed in 1598 he remained in the Netherlands as a soldier for three or four years. Around 1600 Smith left the army and returned to Lincolnshire. There he began to educate himself in history and military strategy, reading about the art of war in the works of Italian politician Niccolò Machiavelli and Roman general Marcus Aurelius. He also perfected his hunting and horsemanship skills with the assistance of Theodore Paleologue, Italian riding master to the Earl of Lincoln. Paleologue was a descendant of Constantine XI , the last Greek emperor of the Eastern Roman Empire. He taught Smith the Italian language and also told him tales about the Ottoman Turks. (Ottoman Turks were Turkish tribes who were part of the Ottoman empire; they were Muslims, or followers of Islam, who sought expansion in Europe in the seventeenth century.) None of these opportunities would have been possible for a man of Smith's station in life without the help of Lord Willoughby.

Describes fantastic adventures

Smith soon left England again, seeking adventure and wealth in the foreign military service. According to his own account he had many exciting adventures—thus presenting a problem for historians. Throughout his life Smith was a prolific writer who gave vivid descriptions of his exploits. Yet modern scholars have questioned his version of events because he seemed primarily interested in self-promotion and advancement. Nevertheless the basic facts of Smith's fantastic tales appear to coincide with other historical records.

In 1600 Smith sailed for Rome with a group of French Catholic pilgrims. His real destination was the Holy Roman Empire, and his purpose was to join the Christian campaign against the Ottoman Turks. Smith wrote that during the voyage he was thrown overboard because he was suspected of being a Huguenot (a member of a branch of Calvinism, a Protestant Christian faith). He said he was then rescued by a pirate or a privateer (people who attach and rob ships), on whose ship he served for some time. After sailing through Italy and Dalmatia he joined the army of the Archduke of Austria. His first encounter with the Ottoman Turks occurred during a relief expedition to a fortified town on the border of western Hungary. He claimed he played a pivotal role in the Christian victory because he had remembered secret signals and diversionary tactics from his reading of military works. As a reward he was promoted to the rank of captain and given command of 250 horsemen.

Sold into slavery

Smith described other feats of bravery he performed while serving under Prince Zsigmond of Transylvania. According to his account, he killed three Turkish soldiers in hand-to-hand combat. As the Europeans were laying siege to a Turkish stronghold in Transylvania, Smith wrote, a Turk challenged them to a duel to the death on horseback. The Europeans drew straws to select their champion (the person who would engage in combat), and Smith won. During the encounter he decapitated (beheaded) this Turk and two others. When the siege ended the Europeans had triumphed. In recognition of Smith's valor, Prince Zsigmond awarded him a coat of arms (an actual coat or an emblem) decorated with three Turk heads to signify his brave feat, then named him "a gentleman."

Smith's next adventure was less successful. The Europeans were soundly defeated at a battle near the Red Tower Pass in Romania. Injured but still alive, Smith was captured and sold into slavery. He lived first in Istanbul, Turkey, where he apparently befriended a Turkish lady. He was then taken to Russia as a slave. In time he killed his master, escaped, and journeyed west until he eventually found Zsigmond. With a present of gold ducats (coins) from his Transylvanian patron, Smith toured Germany, France, and Spain. He reached Gibral-

" . . . had God not blessed the discoverers. . . . "

John Smith's writings provide modern historians with extensive information about early Jamestown, the first successful English settlement in America. In *Generall Historie of Virginia* (1624) Smith described the settlers' arrival on the coast of the Chesapeake Bay in 1606 and their subsequent attempts to build a colony while establishing relations with the Native Americans. Following is an excerpt from that account. (Smith referred to himself in the third person.)

The first land they made they called Cape Henry; where thirty of them recreating themselves on shore, were assaulted by five savages, who hurt two of the English very dangerously.

That night was the box opened, and the orders read, in which Bartholomew Gosnoll, John Smith, Edward Wingfield,

Christopher Newport, John Ratliffe, John Martin, and George Kendall, were named to be the Council, and to choose a President amongst them for a year, who with the Council should govern. Matters of moment were to be examined by a jury, but determined by the major part of the Council, in which the President had two voices.

Until the 13 of May they sought a place to plant in; then the Council was sworn, Master Wingfield was chosen President, and an oration [formal speech] made, why Captain Smith was not admitted of the Council as the rest.

Now fell every man to work, the Council contrive [manage] the Fort, the rest cut down trees to make place to pitch their tents; some provide clapboard to relade [reload] the ships, some make gardens, some nets, etc. The savages often visited us kindly. The Presidents overweening jealousy would admit no

tar, and from there sailed to Tangier and Morocco. After narrowly escaping capture by French pirates, Smith returned home on an English warship.

Joins Virginia Company

Smith arrived in England around 1605. The following year he was briefly involved in a failed plan for an English settlement in Guiana. Then, through connections with the Willoughbys, he met Bartholomew Gosnold, a businessman starting a colony in North America. Smith joined this venture, which was called the Virginia Company, and was named one of seven council members who would oversee the Virginia Colony in America. On December 19, 1606, the party of 105

exercise at arms, or fortification but the boughs [branches] of trees cast together in the form of a half moon by the extraordinary pains and diligence of Captain Kendall.

Newport, Smith, and twenty others, were sent to discover the head of the river: by divers [various] small habitants they passed, in six days they arrived at a town called Powhatan, consisting of some twelve houses, pleasantly seated on a hill; before it three fertile isles, about it many of their cornfields, the place is very pleasant, and strong by nature, of this place the Prince is called Powhatan, and his people Powhatans. To this place the river is navigable: but higher within a mile, by reason of the rocks and Isles, there is not passage for a small boat, this they call The Falls. The people in all parts kindly entreated them, till being returned within twenty miles of James town, they gave just cause of jealousy: but had God not blessed the discoverers otherwise than those at the Fort, there had been an end of that plantation; for at the Fort, where they arrived the next day, they found 17 men hurt, and a boy slain by the savages, and had it not chanced a cross barre [bar] shot from the Ships struck down a bough from a tree amongst them, that caused them to retire, our men would have all been slain since they were all at work and their arms were stored away.

Hereupon the President was contented the Fort should be palisaded [fenced], the ordnance [stock of military supplies] mounted, his men armed and exercised: for many were the assaults, and ambushes of the savages, and our men by their disorderly straggling were often hurt, when the savages by the nimbleness of their heels well escaped.

Reprinted in: Colbert, David, ed. Eyewitness to America. New York: Pantheon Books, 1997, pp. 16–17.

emigrants embarked in three ships from Blackwall, England. For some unknown reason, the names of the council members were sealed in a box that was not to be opened until the expedition reached America. Christopher Newport was temporarily placed in charge during the voyage. The crossing was difficult, and soon Smith came into conflict with Newport over an unspecified issue. Possibly unaware that Smith was a member of the council, Newport had him arrested and imprisoned for the majority of the trip.

Valuable leader at Jamestown

When the party reached Virginia on April 26, 1607, Smith was still under suspicion. Nevertheless he was officially made a councilor of the colony. In addition, his military experience soon made him an invaluable leader of the capital of the colony, which was called Jamestown in honor of King James I . The Jamestown settlers were totally unprepared for surviving in an unfamiliar land. Motivated mainly by stories of an Eldorado (a city full of gold) that could be found in the New World (a term referring to North and South America), they had not acquired the skills to support themselves by farming. Consequently they had to buy, beg, or steal food and other necessities from the Powhatans, the local Native American tribe. It was at this time that the colonists also came to rely on Smith's resourcefulness and business sense. During his stay in Virginia he explored rivers, traded with the Native Americans, made maps, and kept detailed notes that he later published. Smith's writings provided modern historians with extensive information about early Jamestown. Smith was also one of the first Englishmen to regard Native Americans as human beings.

Saved by Pocahontas?

In 1607 Smith was captured while exploring Powhatan territory and taken before Powhatan, the powerful leader of a confederacy of area tribes. According to one of Smith's accounts of the event, the chief's twelve-year-old daughter, Pocahontas, prevented him from executing Smith. In a letter to Queen Anne (wife of James I), dated 1616, Smith claimed that Powhatan sentenced him to death. Then, Smith declared, "at the minute of my execution, [Pocahontas] . . . hazarded the beating out of her own braines to save mine." Some scholars have questioned this version of the incident. In an earlier account, for instance, Smith mentioned neither Pocahontas nor an execution. He simply said he was brought before Powhatan, who questioned him about the presence of the English in Native American territory. After Smith gave his reply, the chief dismissed him. Whatever the truth of the story, Smith managed to survive not only captivity but—unlike many of his fellow colonists—also the diseases that ravished the colony.

Leaves Virginia

By September 1608 Smith was the only councilor remaining in Virginia, so he became president of the colony by

default (automatically). Under his leadership the inexperienced settlers built houses, completed a church, fortified Jamestown, and learned how to farm and fish. While Smith managed to keep the struggling colony from dissolving, however, he did so at the expense of his own popularity. He imposed strict rules and forced the colonists to obey his orders. As a result he caused much resentment and bitterness. In 1609 another group of settlers arrived from England. Along with them came several of

Smith's old enemies, who plotted against him. The colonists also had continuing problems with the Native Americans. Smith might have been able to weather these difficulties if he had not been severely wounded when a stray spark from a fire lit his gunpowder bag as he lay napping. The explosion and subsequent flames burned him so badly that his life was threatened. The following October he sailed back to England.

Explores New England

Smith survived his injuries and reported the colony's progress to the Virginia Company in London. But he would never see Virginia again. In 1614 he sailed to the northeast coast of North America along the Atlantic Ocean, in the area of present-day Cape Cod, Massachusetts. Calling the region New England, he mapped part of the coastline. Smith planned two later excursions to America: one to establish a colony in New England, and the other to go to Plymouth with the *Mayflower* settlers. None of these plans worked out, and Smith never went back to America. Nevertheless, he acquired the title of admiral of New England. He spent his time drafting maps and writing pamphlets. In 1624 the Virginia Company went bankrupt and James I took over Virginia as a royal colony (that is, the colony was administered by the British government instead of private investors). That year Smith published his best-known work, *The Generall Historie of Virginia,* in which he described the first successful attempt at English colonization in America. He also wrote a handbook for sailors. In 1631 Smith published his last work, a discussion of problems in Virginia and New England. He died later that year while visiting at the home of a friend.

For further research

Barbour, Philip L. *The Worlds of Captain John Smith.* Boston: Houghton Mifflin, 1964.

Colbert, David, ed. *Eyewitness to America.* New York: Pantheon Books, 1997, pp. 16–17.

Emerson, Everett H. *Captain John Smith.* Rev. ed. Old Tappan, N.J.: Macmillan Library Reference, 1993.

Foster, Genevieve. *The World of Captain John Smith.* New York: Scribner, 1959.

Graves, Charles P. *John Smith.* Broomall, Pa.: Chelsea House Publishers, 1991.

Hernando de Soto

c. 1500
Extremadura, Spain
May 21, 1542
Mississippi River

First Spanish explorer in the southeastern United States

W hen the Spanish adventurer Hernando de Soto led an expedition along the western coast of Florida in 1539, he was already a seasoned explorer and a wealthy man. He had been drawn to the North American continent by tales of hidden cities containing vast amounts of gold and silver. Although a three-year search for treasure was futile, de Soto and his party possibly became the first Europeans to sight the Mississippi River.

Seeks life of adventure

Hernando de Soto was born around 1500 in Extremadura, a Spanish province near the border of Portugal. Embarking on a life of adventure as a young man, he joined an expedition to Nicaragua led by Spanish explorer Francisco Fernández de Córdoba in 1524. De Soto participated in founding the city of Granada. Sometime after their arrival in Nicaragua, de Soto sided with Córdoba's adversary, Pedro Arias, in a dispute that resulted in Córdoba's death. De Soto then settled in Nicaragua and prospered, partly through his involvement in the slave trade. Once again lured by adventure, however, he

Portrait: Hernando de Soto.
Reproduced by permission of Corbis-Bettmann.

317

joined fellow Spaniard Francisco Pizarro in Pizzaro's third expedition to Peru.

Joins conquest of Peru

When the Spaniards reached Peru in 1531, they began the conquest of the Inca Empire. With its capital at Cuzco, the empire extended thousands of miles. The Spaniards traveled for nearly a year in the Andes, the great South American mountain range. In 1532 they reached the city of Cajamarca, where Atahualpa, the ruler of the Incas, was camped. Pizarro sent de Soto into the city to meet Atahualpa. Feigning friendship, de Soto invited the emperor to dinner and then took him captive.

After imprisoning Atahualpa, Pizarro became the ruler of Peru. Although the Incas staged several uprisings, he stayed in power. During one of the revolts Pizarro ordered the execution of the Incan emperor. Although de Soto protested that Atahualpa's life should be spared, the execution was carried out. In 1533 de Soto joined Pizarro in taking Cuzco, the capital of Peru. During the siege de Soto nearly lost his life in an ambush. He stayed in Peru for three more years before returning to Spain in 1536.

De Soto's participation in the conquest of Peru brought him great wealth and social status. Upon his arrival in Spain, he asked King Charles I to give him an important position in one of Spain's new territories in the Americas. In 1537 the king appointed de Soto the governor of Cuba, granting him the right to conquer and colonize the territory north of Cuba on the mainland of North America (now Florida). First visited by Spanish explorers Juan Ponce de León in 1513, the land was still a vast, unexplored wilderness.

Searches for gold in Florida

De Soto began preparing for his expedition to Florida. In the meantime, Spanish conquistador Álvar Núñez Cabeza de Vaca had returned to Spain after many years of exploring the area that is now Texas. Cabeza de Vaca told of stories he had heard about the great wealth that could be found in the "Seven Cities of Cibola" (see **Francisco de Coronado** and **Estevanico** entries). Supposedly these fabulous cities were somewhere in the southeastern part of North America. De Soto was

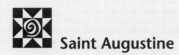

Saint Augustine

In 1539–40 Spanish conquistador Hernando de Soto opened the way for settlement of the North American continent. By the 1560s, however, the Spanish were competing with the French to establish permanent colonies along the east coast of the Atlantic Ocean. In 1562 and 1564, French Huguenots had tried to start settlements on the site of present-day Parris Island, off the coast of South Carolina, and at Fort Caroline (on the mouth of the St. Johns River, near modern-day Jacksonville, Florida). In response to these settlements, Spanish naval officer Pedro Menéndez de Avilés arrived with a fleet off the Atlantic coast, southeast of Jacksonville, in 1565. After driving the French away, he planned to establish a permanent settlement that would protect the area from French invasion. On September 8, 1565, Menéndez and his men stepped ashore and took possession of the territory for Spain. He had planned carefully: he had brought plenty of supplies, and along with him came farmers and carpenters. Although the Spanish settlers managed to build a fort, it was little more than a ditch. They had a miserable winter, and many suffered from disease and starvation. The following spring the Spanish began building a town called Saint Augustine, which was designed using a grid pattern with narrow streets and small blocks. The houses were also narrow and set close together. Thus the Spanish established the oldest city—and the first permanent European settlement—in North America. In 1672 they began constructing the great Castillo de San Marcos, a stone fort that still stands today. Many of the original houses have been preserved, and Saint Augustine has become a popular tourist site.

immediately intrigued by the tales. Although Cabeza de Vaca had failed to find any treasure, de Soto believed that he himself might discover riches in his new territory. He sailed from Spain on April 7, 1538, with six hundred men and two hundred horses. After stopping in Cuba for more supplies, his party landed on the western coast of the Florida peninsula at the site of modern-day Tampa Bay on May 27, 1539.

Six months later the Spaniards reached the town of Apalachen near the present-day city of Tallahassee, Florida. Ignoring a hostile reception from Native Americans, the explorers spent the winter in the area. When spring came, de

Soto and his party left in search of a place called Cofitachequi, which they heard was ruled by a powerful and wealthy queen. In April 1540 they reached Cofitachequi, which was located seventy-five miles north of the Savannah River in territory that is now eastern Georgia. The Spaniards discovered that the city was indeed ruled by a queen, but they were disappointed to learn that her treasure was only a few freshwater pearls (gems that are formed in the shells of oysters).

Follows second false lead

De Soto's party left Cofitachequi two weeks later, moving north to the land of Chiaha, which was also rumored to be rich in gold. In early June, after crossing the Appalachian Mountains, the Spaniards reached Chiaha. Once again they had been led astray: Chiaha turned out to be simply an island (now called Burns Island) in the middle of the Tennessee River, and offered no wealth. From there de Soto led his men south. Along the way they met two great Native American chiefs, Cosa and Tuscaloosa. Cosa lived on the Coosa River north of the site of present-day Childersburg, Alabama. Tuscaloosa lived in a village on the shores of the Alabama River.

At Mabila (possibly near present-day Choctaw Bluff, Alabama) de Soto received word that his ships had sailed into the Gulf of Mexico to meet him. As the Spaniards continued to move southward toward the Gulf, they engaged in a fierce battle with a group of Native Americans. During the conflict they were pushed to the north and west, and thereby forced to set up a winter camp about 125 miles east of the Mississippi River. The following spring they were attacked by members of the Chickasaw tribe, who killed twelve of de Soto's men.

Leaving camp in late April 1541, the Spaniards traveled to present-day Memphis, Tennessee, in early May. By June they were again in search of treasure. This time de Soto had heard rumors of gold and silver in the Ozark Mountains, so he built some barges and crossed the river. He and his men spent several months traveling through the region that is now the state of Arkansas, but they found no treasure. Spending a difficult winter near modern-day Camden, they were in desperate straits by spring. Several men had died. The Spaniards had also lost most of their horses. De Soto decided to turn back and sail down the Mississippi to the Gulf of Mexico.

Dies en route to Gulf

Upon reaching the river, the Spaniards raided a Native American village so they would have a place to build boats for the trip down to the Gulf. During the night of May 21, 1542, however, de Soto fell ill with a fever and died. His men reportedly buried his body in the river so it would not be discovered by Native Americans. Led by a Spanish colleague, Luis de Moscoso, the survivors completed seven barges. In July they went down the Brazos River (in present-day Texas) to the mouth of the Mississippi. Sailing along the Gulf to the settlement of Panuco in northwestern Mexico, they embarked for Spain. It was now September 10, 1543—more than five years since de Soto's expedition had set out for Florida. Of the 600 men in the original party, only 311 had survived. Moreover, their leader had died without ever finding treasure in his new territory. Nevertheless, he is remembered today as the leader of the first European party to sight the Mississippi River. Thus he opened the way for future European exploration in North America.

Hernando de Soto and his party reaching the Mississippi River.
Reproduced by permission of Corbis-Bettmann.

For further research

Duncan, David Ewing. *Hernando de Soto: A Savage Quest in the Americas.* New York: Crown Publishers, 1995.

Montgomery, Elizabeth Rider. *Hernando de Soto.* Champaign, Ill.: Garrard Publishing Company, 1964.

De Soto's Trail thru the Southeast. http://www.conquestchannel.cominset9.html Available July 13, 1999.

Spanish Exploration and Conquest of Native Americans. http://www.conquestchannel.com/ Available July 13, 1999.

Whitman, Sylvia. *Hernando de Soto and the Explorers of the American South.* New York: Chelsea House, 1991.

Squanto

c. 1600
Patuxet (in present-day Massachusetts)
1622
possibly Cape Cod, Massachusetts

Wampanoag translator and guide

Squanto, also known as Tasquantum (or Tisquantum), was a major seventeenth-century Native American figure. He is remembered as the interpreter, guide, and agricultural advisor who shepherded the English settlers of Plymouth Colony through their unstable early existence in the New World (a European term for North America and South America). Squanto was overshadowed, however, by the Pokanoket chief **Massasoit** (see entry), who is famous for establishing a peace treaty with the Pilgrims in 1621. Controversy surrounds Squanto's life because of his attempts to undermine Massasoit's authority. Squanto is nevertheless considered to be the person who did more than anyone else to secure the survival of the Plymouth Colony settlers.

Escapes slavery

Squanto was born around 1600 in Patuxet, a village of about two thousand Native Americans located in what is now Plymouth Bay, Massachusetts. He was a member of the Patuxet band of the Wampanoag tribe, which dominated the region. During Squanto's lifetime this area was visited by European

"Squanto continued with them and was their interpreter, and was a special instrument sent of God for their good beyond their expectation."

Plymouth Colony governor William Bradford.

Portrait: Squanto.
Reproduced by permission of The Granger Collection Ltd.

traders and explorers several times. In fact, French explorer **Samuel de Champlain** (see entry) provided extensive documents of his visits in 1605 and 1606. As a result of this frequent contact, the Patuxets engaged in trade with the constant traffic of traders and explorers. At the time Squanto apparently held the prominent position of chief of the Patuxet tribe.

In 1614 Squanto's life was dramatically changed. During that year, he and twenty other Patuxets were kidnaped by English explorer Thomas Hunt. Taking his captives to Málaga, Spain, Hunt sold them into slavery. Squanto, however, was rescued by Spanish friars (members of a religious order who combine life as a monk with outside religious activity) who wanted to convert the Native Americans to Christianity. While historians are uncertain about Squanto's movements over the next three years, he is known to have arrived in London, England, in 1617. There he resided with John Slaney, the treasurer of the New Foundland Company, who was interested in exploring the New World.

During his time in London, Squanto was immersed in English culture and learned the English language. In 1617 Slaney sent him on an expedition to New Foundland. There Squanto met explorer Thomas Dermer, and the two men returned to England the following year. Squanto may have been an indentured servant (a servant who works for a certain length of time in order to buy his or her freedom) during this time rather than a slave (one who is owned by a master). In serving both Slaney and Dermer, Squanto may have hoped to earn his passage home. In any event, he traveled once again to the New World with Dermer in 1619, this time returning to the Patuxet region of his birth.

Finds Patuxet abandoned

In 1617, during Squanto's absence, a great epidemic (perhaps the plague) swept the Massachusetts Bay region. Because the Native Americans had no immunity (built-in resistance) against European diseases, a majority of them died. The Patuxet band, for instance, was virtually wiped out. Squanto returned in 1619 to find the village of his youth abandoned. The few surviving Native Americans banded together into smaller tribes. Unfortunately, these tribes found it difficult to defend themselves against the Narragansetts and other hostile

Native American groups who had managed to survive the epidemic. The small tribes were also attacked by English and French exploring parties.

Still accompanied by Dermer, Squanto was faced with the task of introducing the Englishman into Wampanoag society. At that time the Native Americans were less than friendly with the English because of recent violence between the two groups. Yet Squanto managed to cultivate relations between Dermer and the Wampanoag. Even the Pokanoket chief Massasoit tolerated Dermer's presence, but this goodwill did not extend to all Native Americans in the area. In 1620 Dermer was killed by warriors who were still hostile to the English, and Squanto was subsequently taken prisoner.

Meets Pilgrims for first time

Another event occurred in 1620, making Squanto an even more prominent historical figure. In November of that year about one hundred Pilgrims (early English settlers who wished to freely practice their own form of Christianity) sailed to the Massachusetts shore aboard a ship called the *Mayflower*. The Pilgrims settled at Patuxet and called their community Plymouth Colony. Because the English knew very little about farming and trade, their first winter in the New World was harsh. As a result, many Pilgrims died of starvation and disease during the winter of 1620–21.

Although they were aware of one another, the Pilgrims and Native Americans did not make contact during that difficult winter. The Pilgrims maintained their distance from their neighbors, even though the Native Americans could have helped them. In turn, the Wampanoags, because of their mixed experiences with Europeans, warily watched the newcomers. Finally, in March 1621, the Pokanokets decided to make contact with the Pilgrims. As leader of the initial welcoming party they chose Samoset, a member of the Abenaki tribe who was familiar with English trading practices and spoke the English language. Squanto was a prominent figure by this time, but he was not nearly so powerful as Massasoit. It was Massasoit who signed the historic treaty of 1621 in which the Wampanoags and the English pledged mutual peace and friendship. (The treaty lasted for forty years.)

Squanto teaches the
Pilgrims to plant corn.
Illustration by C. W. Jeffreys;
Reproduced by permission
of The Granger Collection,
New York.

Symbolizes first Thanksgiving

Luckily, the Pilgrims were receptive to the Native Americans' offers of assistance. Squanto taught the English settlers—most of whom had no knowledge of farming—to plant Indian corn and other vegetables. He also helped to insure the success of their crops by teaching them how to use fish as fertilizer. The English believed the practice of fertilizing with fish to be traditional among the Native Americans. Yet this view has been questioned by historians, some of whom believe that Squanto learned the practice in Europe or New Foundland. Following a bountiful harvest in the fall, the colonists held a three-day feast of celebration, to which they invited Massasoit and ninety of his men. Squanto was reportedly a member of this group. The feast has come to be known as the "first Thanksgiving." Because of his role in teaching the colonists how to grow their own food, Squanto is regarded as the symbol of Native American–Pilgrim cooperation when Thanksgiving is commemorated each year in the United States.

Helps Pilgrims secure settlement

As a reward for his part in peace negotiations, Squanto was sent to live with the Pilgrims. His guidance proved so indispensable that Plymouth governor **William Bradford** (see entry) declared him a "special instrument sent of God for their good." Squanto's role in introducing the English to neighboring Native American tribes was particularly crucial. His extensive travels had provided him with unique qualifications to move freely between the two cultures. Thus it was possible for the colonists to establish vital trade relationships that enabled them to secure seeds and other supplies. They also acquired animal pelts (skins), which they sent to England to repay investments and trade for English goods.

Squanto helps the English

William Bradford, governor of the Plymouth Colony, kept a journal (later published in *Of Plymouth Plantation*) in which he told the story of Squanto:

Anno [year]. 1621

. . . But about the 16. of March a certain Indian came boldly amongst them [the colonists] and spoke to them in broken English, which they could well understand, but marvelled at it. . . . His name was Samoset; he tould them also of another Indian whose name was Squanto, a native of this place, who had been in England & could speak better English than himself. . . . [After the signing of a treaty between the Native Americans and the English] Squanto continued with them and was their interpreter, and was a special instrument sent of God for their good beyond their expectation. He directed them how to set their corn, where to take fish, and to procure other commodities, and was also their pilot to bring them to unknown places for their profit, and never left them till he died. . . .

. . . Then the sickness began to fall sore amongst them, and the weather so bad as they could not make much sooner any dispatch. Againe, the Govr. [Bradford's predecessor, John Carver, who died in April 1621] & chief of them, seeing so many die, and fall down sick daily. . . .

Afterwards they (as many as were able) began to plant their corn, in which service Squanto stood them in great stead, showing them both the manner how to set it, and after how to dress & tend it. Also he tould them except they got fish & set with it (in these old grounds) it would come to nothing, and he showed them that in the middle of April they should have store enough come up the brook, by which they began to build, and taught them how to take it, and where to get other provisions [food supplies] necessary for them; all which they found true by trial & experience. Some English seed they sow, as wheat & peas, but it came not to good, either by the badness of the seed, or lateness of the season, or both, or some other defect.

Reprinted in: Kupperman, Karen Ordahl, ed. Major Problems in American Colonial History. *Lexington, Mass.: D. C. Heath, 1993, pp. 120–21.*

Plots against Massasoit

Despite his important role in establishing friendly relations between the Native Americans and the English, Squanto was a controversial figure. According to some reports, he tried to increase his status among the Native Americans by exaggerating his influence with the English. He also alarmed neighboring tribes with reports that colonists kept a plague (a deadly disease)—he may actually have meant gunpowder—buried underground so that it could be released at any time. There is also evidence that he tried to undermine Massasoit's relationship with the English. A crisis developed in 1622 when Squanto attempted to trick the English by telling them Massasoit was plotting with the hostile Narragansett tribe to launch an attack and destroy the Plymouth Colony.

When Squanto's secret plan was discovered, Massasoit demanded that he be executed. The Plymouth settlers were also angry with Squanto. In fact, Bradford admitted to Massasoit that Squanto deserved death for his act of betrayal. However, it was a measure of the colonists' dependence on Squanto that they protected him from Massasoit's revenge. In November 1622, additional English settlers arrived in the Plymouth Colony. Like the original Pilgrims, they came ill-prepared for the approaching New England winter. Squanto guided an expedition of Plymouth settlers to trade with Cape Cod Native Americans for corn. He fell ill with what Bradford described as "Indian fever" and died within a few days. According to Bradford, the dying Squanto expressed his wish to "go to the Englishmen's God in Heaven" and "bequeathed his little property to his English friends, as remembrances of his love."

For further research
Dubowski, Cathy East. *The Story of Squanto: First Friend of the Pilgrims*. Milwaukee: Gareth Stevens Publishers, 1997.

Kupperman, Karen Ordahl, ed. *Major Problems in American Colonial History*. Lexington, Mass.: D. C. Heath, 1993, pp. 120–21.

Stevenson, Augusta. *Squanto: Young Indian Hunter*. Indianapolis: Bobbs-Merrill. 1962.

Peter Stuyvesant

c.1610
Scherpenzeel, Netherlands
1672
Manhattan, New York

Dutch director general of New Netherland

Peter Stuyvesant was the colorful and controversial director general of the Dutch colony of New Netherland (present-day New York State). During his seventeen years in office, he caused considerable unrest by imposing heavy taxes and passing laws that prohibited religious freedom. However, Stuyvesant was also responsible for some important progress in the colony, such as improving relations with nearby English settlements and promoting commerce. Nevertheless citizens of New Amsterdam (now New York City) ultimately forced him to declare the city a municipality (self-governing political unit). Stuyvesant's harsh rule eventually led to the downfall of New Netherland, which was taken over by the English with no resistance from the Dutch in 1664.

Seeks adventure

Petrus Stuyvesant (called Peter by the English) was born in 1592. His mother died in 1625, and his father, the Reverend Balthazar Johannes Stuyvesant, remarried two years later. Before his mother's death, Peter lived with his family in Scherpenzeel (now in West Stellingwerf), where his father was

" . . . if any one should [appeal a law], I will make him a foot shorter, and send the pieces to Holland, and let him appeal in that way."

Peter Stuyvesant.

Portrait: Peter Stuyvesant.
Reproduced by permission of The Library of Congress.

pastor of the Dutch Reformed Church. (The Dutch Reformed Church was a branch of Calvinism, a Protestant Christian faith based on the concept of a church-dominated state.) After remarrying, the Reverend Stuyvesant was assigned to a parish at Delfzyl in Groningen. Peter had two half-brothers, two half-sisters, and a full sister.

Always an adventurous person, Stuyvesant entered the military in order to serve his country both at home and abroad. In 1635 he joined the Dutch West India Company in Brazil, where he remained for nine years. The Dutch West India Company was a privately owned enterprise that promoted trade and settlement in the New World, the European term for North America and South America. Then, in 1643, Stuyvesant was appointed governor of Dutch possessions in Curaçao (an island in the Caribbean Sea) and the Leeward Islands (a chain of islands in the Pacific Ocean near Hawaii). In 1644 Stuyvesant used his military training when he led an expedition against the French and Spanish on Saint Martin, one of the Leeward Islands. The attack was waged in March, with the final siege taking place on April 16. During the battle Stuyvesant was shot in his right leg, which had to be amputated. Contrary to legend, his leg was buried in Curaçao, not in Holland. He returned to Holland to recuperate and to be fitted with an artificial limb. In keeping with Stuyvesant's flamboyant personality, the limb became known as his "silver leg" because he decorated it with many adornments. In 1645 he married Judith Bayard in the Walloon Church of Breda, where her father had been minister of the congregation for years. The couple had two sons.

Becomes director general

In 1645, Stuyvesant went before the Zealand Chamber of the Dutch West India Company and requested a commission to go to New Netherland. Less than a year later he was officially appointed director general of New Netherland and the islands of Curaçao, Buen Aire (now Bonaire), and Aruba (all located in the Caribbean Sea off the coast of Venezuela). On Christmas Day 1646, Stuyvesant set sail for his new destination with his wife, his widowed sister, and her three sons. The party of four vessels, carrying countless soldiers, servants, and adventurers, was ordered by Stuyvesant to stop first in

"Stuyvesant's Bad Government"

Junker van der Donck, formerly a lawyer in the Netherlands, served on a committee that reported on conditions in the New Netherland colony. He correctly predicted that mismanagement would eventually doom New Netherland; for in 1664, seventeen years after Peter Stuyvesant was appointed governor, the colony was taken over by the British during a peaceful invasion. Following is an excerpt from van der Donck's scathing description of Stuyvesant's arrival in New Amsterdam in 1647.

Stuyvesant's first arrival—for what passed on the voyage is not for us to speak of—was like a peacock, with great state and pomp. The appellation of Lord General, and similar titles, were never before known here. Almost every day he caused proclamations of various import to be published, which were for the most part never observed, and have long since been a dead letter, except the Fine excise [tax], *as that yielded a profit. . . . At one time, after leaving the house of the minister, where the consistory [church governing body] had been sitting and had risen, it happened that Arnoldous Van Herdenbergh related the proceedings relative to the estate of Zeger Teunisz, and how he himself, as curator [caretaker], had appealed from the sentence; whereupon the Director [Stuyvesant], who had been sitting there with them as an elder [church official], interrupted him and replied, "It may during my administration be contemplated to appeal, but if any one should do it, I will make him a foot shorter, and send the pieces to Holland, and let him appeal in that way." In our opinion this country will never flourish under the government of the Honorable Company [Dutch West India Company], but will pass away and come to an end of itself, unless the Honorable Company be reformed.*

Reprinted in: Colbert, David, ed. *Eyewitness to America*. New York: Pantheon Books, 1997, pp. 28–29.

Curaçao. They stayed at the island for a few weeks, and then sailed on to New Amsterdam, where they anchored on May 11, 1647. Stuyvesant's critics said he arrived "like a peacock, with great state and pomp" (see box).

Prohibits religious freedom

Stuyvesant wasted no time in utilizing his authority. By May 27 he had appointed a naval commander as well as a superintendent of naval equipment. This was the beginning of his preparation for an expedition against the Spanish, who were operating within the confines of the Dutch West India

Company's chartered territory. The first ordinance he enacted after his arrival was a direct reflection of his personal politics: it prohibited the sale of intoxicants and decreed the observance of Sunday as a religious day. This led to his appointment as a church warden on July 22, when he took it upon himself to oversee the reorganization of the Dutch Reformed Church in New Amsterdam. As a son of one minister and the son-in-law of another, Stuyvesant had rigid ideas about religion. He was a strict follower of the Reformed Church and had little tolerance for liberal (free-thinking) religious views.

Within nine years Stuyvesant had gained the full support of like-minded clergymen and the governing council. On February 1, 1656, Stuyvesant issued a harsh ordinance that prohibited meetings and gatherings of people who were not members of the Dutch Reformed Church. This made it nearly impossible for other religious groups to assemble and worship. Although Stuyvesant's order was aimed mainly at Lutherans, it affected Quakers and other groups as well. The following June the directors of the Dutch West India Company in Amsterdam asked Stuyvesant to be more lenient, because the rule was resented by many of the settlers. Their plea landed on deaf ears, and the ordinance stayed in place throughout the Dutch regime in New Netherland.

Citizens demand change

Stuyvesant did make some progress during his career as director general, perhaps as a result of his stern approach to government. He promoted friendly relations with English settlements, drove the Swedes out of Delaware, and increased commerce in the region. Nevertheless, his harsh, dictatorial rule proved to be his downfall. Despite instituting a Board of Nine Men to improve everyday life in New Netherland, hard times fell upon the colony. Unhappy and tired of living under harsh rule, citizens of New Amsterdam pressured Stuyvesant to make the city a municipality (a self-governing political unit). On July 28, 1649, representatives of the people drew up a document titled "Remonstrance," which detailed Stuyvesant's handling of contraband (smuggled goods) he sold arms to Native American tribes. The document also charged Stuyvesant with seizing land for nonpayment of taxes, despite the fact that many landowners were unable to pay because of the economic impact of a recent war. The people felt that New Netherland had no chance of becoming as economically prosperous as Virginia or New England because it was established solely for the benefit of the Dutch West India Company. They won their case on February 3, 1653, when New Amsterdam was declared a municipality. Stuyvesant retained all of his power, however, and the proclamation did very little to change the structure of the colonial government.

New Netherland falls to English

Fearing war with England, the following year Stuyvesant summoned representatives from other New Netherland settlements, hoping for economic support. When no money was offered he merely imposed additional taxes on land, livestock, and rents. Stuyvesant wanted to finish the fortifications before the English invasion. His efforts were in vain. James, Duke of York (later King James II), the younger brother of the English King Charles II, wanted to expand the English kingdom. The New World, especially areas under Dutch rule, became James's main target. This plan was agreeable to Charles, who would profit from yearly taxes on the new territory. On March 12, 1664, Charles issued a charter that granted James rights to all territory between the Connecticut and Delaware Rivers. In addition, James would be able to establish laws and taxes as long as they agreed with English laws. On August 18, 1664, four hundred English troops, several frigates (battleships), and a bomb easily intimidated Stuyvesant's forces. The Dutch surrendered peacefully in only nine days, but the terms of surrender were very generous. The property of New Netherland landowners was protected, and anyone wishing to leave had a year to do so. New settlers from Holland would be admitted, and Dutch inheritance laws would be respected. In fact, many New Netherland citizens felt they were better off under English rule than they had been under Stuyvesant. Within a short time New Netherland was renamed New York, and New Amsterdam became New York City.

After losing his colony, Stuyvesant withdrew from public life. In 1665 he went back to the Netherlands to defend his official conduct. He then returned to New York and settled on a farm that had been given to him in 1650 by the directors of the Dutch West India Company. He lived there until his death in 1672, and was buried under the chapel he had built on his farm. The chapel is still standing in Manhattan, and it is now known as St. Mark's Episcopal Church. In 1922 the two hundred fiftieth anniversary of Stuyvesant's death was commemorated at the church.

For further research

Colbert, David, ed. *Eyewitness to America.* New York: Pantheon Books, 1997, pp. 28–29.

Crouse, Anna, and Russel Crouse. *Peter Stuyvesant of Old New York.* New York: Random House Books for Young Adults, 1963.

De Leeuw, Adéle. *Peter Stuyvesant.* Champaign, Ill.: Garrard Publishing Company, 1970.

Quackenbush, Robert. *Old Silver Leg Takes Over: A Story of Peter Stuyvesant.* Paramus, N.J.: Prentice Hall, 1986.

Edward Taylor

1642
Sketchley, England
June 24, 1729
Westfield, Massachusetts

Puritan minister and poet

Edward Taylor was a Puritan minister in Westfield, Massachusetts, who wrote poetry to express his religious inspiration and beliefs. (Puritans were a Christian group who observed strict moral and spiritual codes.) The only verses by Taylor that appeared in print during his lifetime, however, were two stanzas from "Upon Wedlock & Death of Children" (1682 or 1683), which Puritan minister **Cotton Mather** (see entry) included in his book *Right Thoughts in Sad Hours* (1689). His work was virtually unknown until scholars discovered and published his poetry in the twentieth century. Yet today he is considered a major American poet, and his more than two hundred *Poetical Meditations* (1682–25) have been called the most important poetic achievements of colonial America. Although he accepted the stern beliefs of his fellow Puritans, he often focused on God's grace (good will) and the experience of religious ecstasy (joy) and that spirit is reflected in his verse.

Seeks religious freedom

Edward Taylor was born in Sketchley, England, around 1642. Little is known about his early life, but scholars assume

" . . . Is this thy play,/ To spin a web out of thyself/To catch a fly?/ For why?"

From Edward Taylor's poem "Upon a Spider Catching a Fly."

his parents were dissenters (Protestants who rebelled against the practices of the Church of England, the official religion of the country). Nevertheless, Taylor apparently did not experience persecution as a result of his family's beliefs while he was growing up. Although he supposedly went to Cambridge University, there is no record of his attendance. In addition, his religion prevented him from taking the oath of loyalty to the Church of England that was required of all Cambridge students. Taylor must have received an education, however, for he later wrote that he was a teacher in rural England during the mid-1660s.

In 1668 Taylor decided to join other Puritans in seeking religious freedom in the American colonies. Leaving his home and family, he set sail for the Massachusetts Bay Colony. Upon his arrival he contacted Puritan leader Increase Mather (see box in Cotton Mather entry) and John Hull, master of the Massachusetts mint (government agency that prints money). Through these connections Taylor was able to study for the ministry at Harvard College. When he graduated with a bachelor of arts degree in 1671 he accepted a position as the only minister in Westfield, Massachusetts, a town on the frontier about a hundred miles away from Harvard. In 1674 Taylor married Elizabeth Fitch, and after her death he wed Ruth Wyllys in 1692. With his two wives he had fourteen children, most of whom he outlived.

Portrays benevolent God

Taylor remained in Westfield for the rest of his life—fifty-eight years. During the late 1670s he began writing poetry, and he continued to compose verses until shortly before his death. Like other Puritan poets, he used plain, everyday images such as a spider catching a fly or a "sweeping flood" to convey the power of God. He also described the universe as a "Bowling Alley" in which the Creator (God) is a sportsman who rolls the sun into its place. Other images depicted God as a designer hanging the "Tapistry" of the world's landscape and lighting the sky with "twinckling Lanthorns [twinkling lanterns]." Twentieth-century scholars, who discovered Taylor's manuscripts in the 1930s, have organized his work in three distinct groups according to chronology and themes.

Taylor completed his first collection of poems, a total of thirty-five, which he gave the title *God's Determinations touching his Elect,* in the early 1680s. With this group, his main theme is that a forgiving God presides over the battle between Christ (the embodiment of goodness) and Satan (the Devil, or the ultimate evil force) for control of the elect (Christians who are chosen by God for salvation, or forgiveness of all sins). By portraying a loving and merciful God, Taylor differed dramatically from his fellow Puritans, who constantly warned their congregations that an angry God would doom them to eternal suffering—in the fiery furnace of the underworld—if they did not repent (feel regret) for their sins. For instance, the most popular clergyman-poet of the day, Michael Wigglesworth, wrote *The Day of Doom.* In this collection of verses he attempted to frighten his readers into seeking forgiveness from God.

Composes occasional poems

Taylor's second group of poems consists of occasional verses (poems for special occasions), which were probably written in the 1680s. Departing from great theological (religious theory) issues, he wrote about common human experiences to express his faith. For instance, in "Upon Wedlock, & Death of Children," he showed how love between husband and wife is strengthened through the loss of children. Grief leads to a better understanding of divine will. In "Upon a Spider Catching a Fly" he portrayed the "dance of death" between a spider, a fly, and a wasp. The poem symbolizes the human predicament: the sinner (the "silly fly") risks being caught by Satan ("Hell's spider"), while the person who is saved (the wasp) has the strength to escape Satan's web.

 A best-seller

Edward Taylor is now considered a major American poet, but his unpublished verses were not discovered until the twentieth century. The most popular poet during Taylor's lifetime was Michael Wigglesworth, a clergyman whose book *The Day of Doom* (1662) became a best-seller. By 1751 *The Day of Doom* had gone through seven editions. The sixth edition of his popular second book, *Meat Out of the Eater* (1670), was published in 1721. Wigglesworth's works were so often read and reread that no copies of the first edition of either book have survived. His verse sermons did not appeal to later generations, but his contemporaries admired and heeded his dire predictions. Wigglesworth warned that hellfires awaited "whining hypocrites, Idolaters, false worshippers,/Prophaners of Gods Name, Blasphemers lewd, and Swearers shrewd,/Scoffers at Purity, Sabbath-polluters, Saints persecuters,/ Presumptuous men and proud"—and a whole array of other sinners bound for eternal damnation.

"Upon a Spider Catching a Fly"

In "Upon a Spider Catching a Fly" Edward Taylor portrayed the "dance of death" between a spider, a fly, and a wasp. The poem symbolizes the human predicament: the sinner (the "silly fly") risks being caught by Satan ("Hell's spider"), while the person who is saved (the wasp) has the strength to escape Satan's web.

Thou sorrow, venom [poison] elf.
Is this thy play,
To spin a web out of thyself
To catch a fly?
For why?
I saw a pettish [angry] wasp
Fall foul therein.
Whom yet thy whorl pins [pins on a
    spinning wheel] did not clasp
Lest he should fling
His sting.
But as afraid, remote
Didst stand here at
And with thy little fingers stroke
And gently tap.
His back.
Thou gently him didst treat
Lest he should pet [grow angry],
And in a froppish [irritable], waspish heat
Should greatly fret
Thy net.
Whereas the silly fly,
Caught by its leg

Thou by the throat tookst hastily
And 'hind the head
Biter dead.
This goes to pot, that not
Nature [natural reason] doth call.
Strive not above what strength hath got
Lest in the brawl
Thou fall.
This fray seems thus to us.
Hell's spider gets
His intrails [internal organs] spun to whip
    cords thus.
And wove to nets
And sets [snares].
To tangle Adam's race [humans]
In's [his] stratigems
To their destructions, spoil'd, made base
By venom things
Damn'd sins.
But mighty, gracious Lord
Communicate
Thy grace to break the void, afford
Us glory's gate
And state.
We'll nightingale sing like
When perched on high
In glory's cage, thy glory, bright.
And thankfully,
For joy.

Reprinted in Elliott, Emory, and others, eds. **American** **Literature: A Prentice Hall Anthology.** *Englewood Cliffs, New Jersey, 1991, pp. 160–61.*

Produces best work

Taylor's greatest contribution to American literature was his third group of poems, which he titled *Preparatory Meditations Before My Approach to the Lord's Supper.* Numbering nearly two hundred, the verses in this collection are remarkable for being distinctly non-Puritan. Again, the poet depicted a loving God who is willing to forgive sinners. Taylor composed the verses in *Meditations* to prepare himself to give communion to his congregation, and the poems reveal his spiritual journey through the world. Reflecting on his love for God, he meditated on God's equally strong love for humankind: it is "matchless . . . filling Heaven to the brim!" Taylor continued writing poetry until 1725, only four years before his death. He composed his verses primarily for personal purposes, so colonial Americans did not read his work. Yet Taylor's poetry is valued today not only for its literary merit but also for its glimpses into the gentler, more human side of the Puritan spirit.

For further research

"Edward Taylor" in *The Puritans: American Literature Colonial Period (1608-1700)*. http://www.falcon.jmu.edu/-ramseyil/amicol.htm Available July 13, 1999.

Elliott, Emory, and others, eds. *American Literature: A Prentice Hall Anthology.* Englewood Cliffs, N.J., 1991, pp. 160–61.

Grabo, Norman S. *Edward Taylor.* New York: Twayne Publishers, 1962.

Silverman, Kenneth, ed. *Colonial American Poetry.* New York: Hafner, 1968.

Stanford, Donald E. *Edward Taylor.* Minneapolis, Minn.: University of Minnesota Press, 1965.

Catherine (Kateri) Tekakwitha

1656
Ossernenon (Auriesville), New York
1680
Kanawake, Quebec

Mohawk Catholic nun and candidate
for sainthood

Portrait: Kateri Tekakwitha.
Reproduced by permission of
UPI/Corbis-Bettmann.

Catherine (Kateri) Tekakwitha was the first Native American to be venerated (the first step toward being declared a saint) by the Roman Catholic Church. (The Roman Catholic Church is a branch of Christianity based in Rome, Italy. It is headed by a pope who oversees bishops, priests, and other religious officials.) Because of her peaceful religious nature, she was known as "Lily of the Mohawks." Tekakwitha was born in 1656 in Ossernenon (Auriesville), New York, to a Mohawk father and a Christianized Algonquin mother who had been captured by Mohawks about 1653. At the time there was extensive fighting among Native factions (rival groups) and Europeans in order to acquire more territory in the New World (the European term for North America and South America). Tekakwitha was born into this chaotic atmosphere of tribal warfare and Native American cultural and religious battles with Europeans.

Although the French Jesuits (a Roman Catholic order for men) were making some headway in their attempts to Christianize and colonize New France (parts of present-day Canada and upper New York State), Native Americans remained hostile toward the French. The sixteen-year interval between 1632 and 1648 was reportedly the worst period for the mission. Eight Jesuits were brutally murdered between 1642 and 1649, three by Mohawks from Tekakwitha's village. The Mohawks were known for their violence among the Five Nations (the Iroquois Confederacy, formed around 1570; an alliance of the Mohawks, Senecas, Cayugas, Oneidas, and Onondagas).

Family dies from smallpox

In 1642, eleven years prior to the capture of Tekakwitha's mother, a Jesuit missionary named Isaac Jogues had been taken prisoner by a band of Mohawk warriors and brought to Ossernenon. Like the other Jesuit missionaries he was pressured by French officials to convert the Native Americans and bring them under French rule. Jogues encouraged the tribe to believe that the articles used in the Catholic mass (religious service), including the altar (a structure that serves as the center of the service), were powerful tools of sorcery (witchcraft) and magic. He reportedly also threatened to use his powers to bring death to the tribe if they did not accept Catholicism.

Some years later Jogues went back to France. Upon his return to Ossernenon, he found that a smallpox epidemic (outbreak of a fatal viral disease) had devastated the village. When the Mohawks saw Jogues they killed him with a war axe because they thought he had fulfilled his promise to destroy them. The epidemic took the lives of Tekakwitha's mother, father, and youngest brother. Orphaned at the age of four, she was left disfigured and visually impaired by the disease. She went to live with the family of her uncle, who was a prominent village chief and the husband of her mother's sister. Tekakwitha's uncle was violently opposed to Christianity.

Resists marriage

In 1667 the French government sent a military expedition to avenge the murders of the Jesuit missionaries, including Jogues. After extensive conflict the Mohawks were forced to accept the presence of the missionaries. Although Tekakwitha's uncle did not approve of Christianity, he was obliged to host three missionaries who were sent to Ossernenon. Tekakwitha, who was then eleven, was given the task of looking after them during their short stay. The young girl was reportedly impressed by the gentle, courteous behavior of the Jesuits. Two of the three missionaries later returned to the area to settle and continue their work.

During this time Tekakwitha had reached the customary age for marriage but, according to missionary reports, she refused all romantic advances and any attempt to find her a husband. Her family responded to her resistance with violence and extreme deprivation, such as withholding meals and threatening her life. Possibly Tekakwitha's resistance to the idea of marriage was influenced by Christianized Algonquins and Hurons, who now made up two-thirds of the village. They may have told her about unwed Ursuline nuns (women who belong to a Catholic religious order) in Quebec.

The Mohawks had not traditionally been opposed to the idea of virginity (having no experience with sexual intercourse) and chastity (refraining from sexual relations). In fact, they believed that virginity could bestow great powers, and one Mohawk band had special virgin groups who followed specific codes of behavior. However, evidence suggests that the Mohawks had been greatly shamed when the virgins broke their vows. Europeans contributed to the situation when they introduced alcohol to the Native Americans. Unaccustomed to the effects of drinking liquor, virgins embarrassed themselves and the villagers by violating behavioral codes. Therefore the elders disbanded the group. This incident undoubtedly had an effect on surrounding villages, including Ossernenon.

Converts to Christianity

The story of Tekakwitha's conversion to Christianity was told by a Jesuit missionary named Lamberville. He reported finding the nineteen-year-old in her dwelling, unable to work because of a foot injury. By all accounts she was ordinarily an industrious, willing worker. Lamberville wrote, "I conversed with her about Christianity and I found her so docile that I exhorted her to be instructed and to frequent the chapel, which she did." He further observed "that she had none of the vices of the girls of her age, that encouraged me to teach her henceforth." Tekakwitha then attended his catechism class (instruction in the Catholic religion) through the summer and winter.

A Jesuit missionary, like the one who visited Tekakwitha's village, preaching to Native Americans in New France (Canada) in the seventeenth century. *Reproduced by permission of The Granger Collection Ltd.*

Lamberville was so impressed with Tekakwitha's progress that he baptized her the following Easter, in 1676, earlier than usual for new converts. Tekakwitha was twenty years old. She then received the name Kateri as her baptism name. For six months she remained in her village, enduring ridicule and scorn for her open practice of Christianity. She was accused of sorcery and repeatedly confronted during her trips to and from the chapel. She was also deprived of food on Sundays and Christian holidays when she chose not to work. Once, when she was on her way to the chapel, a Mohawk warrior held a war axe over her head and threatened to kill her. Her aunt also accused her of trying to seduce her uncle (persuade him to engage in sexual relations).

Flees to Canada

Lamberville advised Tekakwitha to leave the village and join the Jesuit mission of Saint Francis Xavier in Kanawake, Quebec, on the Straits of Saint Louis. Formed in 1667 in reaction to the disastrous effects of alcohol on the Iroquois, Kanawake was known for the discipline of its inhabitants. When three Native American converts from the mission were recruiting in Ossernenon, Tekakwitha left with them. At the time of Tekakwitha's departure her uncle was absent from the village. Upon learning of her absence, he vowed to have her and the three converts killed. He set out in pursuit of the party but they eluded him.

When Tekakwitha reached the mission, she was entrusted with the spiritual care of Anastasie Tegonhatsiongo, a former friend of her mother. Tekakwitha received intensive Christian training and proved to be a gifted student. Within months of her arrival she was allowed to receive communion (a Christian religious ceremony in which church members eat bread and drink wine that represent, respectively, the body and blood of Jesus of Nazareth, the founder of Christianity). Anastasie and many others at the mission were opposed to Tekakwitha's desire to remain a virgin. They pressured her to marry, reminding her that with a husband she would be financially secure. However, Tekakwitha resisted their efforts and instead befriended two other women at the mission.

Founds Native American cloister

After visiting the nuns of Hotel-Dieu hospital in Ville-Marie (present-day Montreal) and learning of their ascetic (strict self-denying) practices, Tekakwitha and her two friends decided to form a cloister (home for nuns) for Native Americans. As a final resort, Anastasie asked one of the head priests, Father Cholenic, to assist the women in their project. Although Cholenic and other Catholic authorities considered the idea premature, Tekakwitha was allowed to take a vow of chastity on the Feast of the Assumption in 1679. In addition to her self-imposed restrictions, her life at the mission had its hardships. Her half-sister later charged her with having sexual relations with her husband during an annual winter hunting expedition. After the incident Tekakwitha no longer participated in the hunt. Instead she remained at the mission, where she increased her religious activities.

Observes strict penance

One of the most pronounced features of Tekakwitha's Catholicism was her frequent penances (self-punishments).

She consumed very little food, and what she did eat was often mixed with ashes. Tekakwitha was known to stand barefoot for hours in the snow at the foot of a cross, saying the rosary (chanting prayers while fingering the beads of a necklace attached to a crucifix, or cross). She once spent three continuous nights on a bed of thorns. She also asked a companion to regularly whip her, and she knelt for several hours on her bare knees in an unheated chapel during severe winter weather. Onlookers were amazed at the severity of her practices, which priests attributed to virtue and holy dedication.

Beatified by church

Tekakwitha's devotion to penance probably cut her life short. Her health declined rapidly, and she died at age twenty-four during Holy Week (the week before Easter Sunday). The last Sacraments (religious observance for the dying) were administered at her bedside rather than in the chapel. Tekakwitha is said to have promised intercession (offering of prayers on the behalf of) for those present at her death. According to some reports, shortly before she died her badly disfigured face became radiant with beauty and all scarring completely disappeared.

Miraculous cures of the sick have been credited to Tekakwitha since her death. In recognition of these miracles and her life of piety (dutifulness in religion) and devotion, the Jesuits submitted a petition for her canonization (declaration of sainthood) in 1884. In 1932 her name was formally presented to the Vatican (the seat of the Catholic Church in Rome), and eleven years later she was venerated (given the first of three degrees of holiness). In 1980 Tekakwitha was beatified (declared blessed), thus achieving the second degree of holiness.

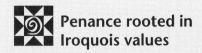

Penance rooted in Iroquois values

Catherine Tekakwitha's strict observance of frequent penances is said to have been rooted in Iroquois spirituality. Placing great value on dreaming, the Iroquois considered dreams to be the language of the soul and extremely important for a functioning society. All members of the community ritualized, interpreted, and acted upon their dreams. They believed that depriving the soul of dreaming would cause sickness. If people did not or could not dream, Iroquois culture provided ceremonial methods for producing a trance state that would put them in touch with the soul. Among the practices were taking a sweat-bath, fasting, singing, chanting, and performing self-mutilations. Food was sometimes mixed with ashes. Alcohol also became part of the rituals after it was introduced by Europeans.

At least fifty biographies and numerous pamphlets have been written about Tekakwitha. More than one hundred articles have examined her life and influence. Her story has also been told in radio broadcasts, film and television dramatizations, two operas, and several plays. These portrayals draw mainly on the accounts of Father Cholenic and Father Chaucheterie, another priest at Kanawake, both of whom claimed to have observed her life of piety. At least one modern scholar, however, claims that Tekakwitha did not exist and that the Jesuits created her to promote their missionary efforts. Nevertheless, many Catholics continue to believe she was an actual person. Two American magazines are devoted to Tekakwitha, keeping a record of favors granted through her help. More than ten thousand Americans are involved in gathering support for her canonization. Eighty-four organizations—camps, clubs, and missions—have been dedicated to Tekakwitha or named in her honor. An international Kateri Tekakwitha movement has been dedicated to establishing a unique form of Native American Catholicism.

For further research

Blessed Kateri Tekakwitha. http://www.knight.org/advent/cathen/14471a .htm Available July 13, 1999.

Brown, Evelyn M. *Kateri Tekakwitha: Mohawk Maid.* San Francisco: Ignatius Press, 1991.

Fisher, Lillian M. *Kateri Tekakwitha: The Lily of the Mohawks.* Boston: Pauline Books and Media, 1996.

James, Edward T., and others, eds. *Notable American Women,* Volume III. Cambridge, Mass.: Belknap Press of Harvard University Press, 1971, pp. 436–37.

Maria van Cortlandt van Rensselaer

July 20, 1645
New Amsterdam (later New York City)
January 24, 1689
Albany, New York

Overseer of Rensselaerswyck

M aria van Cortlandt van Rensselaer was an upper-class housewife who lived in the Dutch colony of New Amsterdam (which later became New York after being taken over by the English). When her husband died she became the overseer (manager or supervisor) of his family's estate to protect her children's inheritance. Van Rensselaer was raised in the tradition of seventeenth-century women in the Netherlands, who were considered the most independent in Europe. This independence was the result of being educated and trained to manage household accounts so they were able to take over the family business if they were ever widowed. Dutch women in the New World (a European term for North America and South America) were also expected to protect the family's wealth so that their children would have an inheritance. Maria van Cortlandt van Rensselaer fulfilled these expectations. Thus she was able to keep secure for her children one of the largest estates in New York.

> "This lady was polite, quite well informed, and of good life and disposition."
>
> *Dutch travel writer Jasper Dankaerts.*

Marries into prominent family

Maria van Cortlandt was born on July 20, 1645, the daughter of the wealthy New Amsterdam (later New York City)

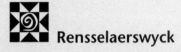

Rensselaerswyck

In 1629 the Dutch West India Company (an enterprise founded to promote colonization in America) realized that in order to attract settlers to the New World, it would need wealthy investors. Among those who came forward was one of the directors of the organization, Kiliaen van Rensselaer. He was awarded a large land grant that formed the basis of Rensselaerswyck, an estate located in the area of present-day Albany, New York (on the Hudson River, about 160 miles north of New York City). Van Rensselaer himself never visited America, but the care of Rensselaerswyck was entrusted to his sons, who made the long journey across the Atlantic Ocean to become managers of the estate. Most important, they guarded title to the land against other speculators (interested buyers). The van Rensselaers lived at the fur-trading post of Fort Orange. In 1654 Jeremias van Rensselaer, the younger son of Kiliaen by a second marriage, settled in America. In 1662 Jeremias married Maria van Cortlandt and took her to live at Rensselaerswyck. They remained on the estate for the rest of their lives.

merchant Oloffe Stevense van Cortlandt and Anna Loockermans. In 1662 she married Jeremias van Rensselaer. When Jeremias proposed to Maria, she was considered too young to marry (she was seventeen). Yet Jeremias felt she was mature enough to manage a household. As he explained in a letter to his mother, "You may think perhaps that she is still a little young and therefore not well able to take care of a household. She is only entering her eighteenth year, but nevertheless we get along very well in the household." He had actually been patient: "I had been thinking of her already a year or two before, when now and then I did an errand at the Manahatans." After they were married, the young couple left for Albany. They settled in the patroon house (home of the Dutch proprietor, or head of the colony), which was the best dwelling at Rensselaerswyck, consisting of two cellars, two rooms, and an attic.

Widowed with six children

The Dutch placed great importance on family and looked forward to the birth of children. In May 1663 Jeremias wrote to his brother in Holland: "You may perhaps be longing to hear whether we have any baby yet. My answer is no, but that my wife is pregnant and that, please God, she will be in childbirth in two or three months at the longest." Maria gave birth to Kiliaen, named for his grandfather, the following August. When Jeremias died in 1674 Maria was responsible for the care of five children under the age of eleven, and she was pregnant with her sixth child. After giving birth she became lame and had to walk with crutches for the rest of her life.

A visit with Maria van Rensselaer

In 1680 Dutch travel writer Jasper Dankaerts called on Maria van Rensselaer at her estate, Rensselaerswyck, near present-day Albany, New York. Dankaerts gave the following account of their visit:

We went to call upon a certain Madam Rentselaer, widow of the Heer Rentselaer, son of the Heer Rentselaer of the colony named the colony of Rentselaerswyck, comprising twelve miles square from Fort Orange, that is, twenty-four miles square in all. She is still in possession of the place, and still administers it as patroonesse [female patroon, or proprietor], until one Richard van Rentselaer, residing at Amsterdam, shall arrive in the country, whom she expected in the summer, when he would assume the management of it himself. This lady was polite, quite well informed, and of good life and disposition. She had experienced several proofs of the Lord [had religious experiences]. The breaking up of the ice had once carried away her entire mansion, and every thing connected with it, of which place she had made too much account. Also, in some visitations of her husband, death, and others before. In her last child-bed, she became lame or weak in both of her sides, so that she had to walk with two canes or crutches. In all these trials, she had borne herself well, and God left not Himself without witness in her. She treated us kindly, and we ate here exceedingly good pike, perch, and other fish, which now began to come and be caught in great numbers. We had several conversations with her about the truth, and practical religion, mutually satisfactory. We went to look at several of her mills at work, which she had there on an ever-running stream, grist-mills, saw-mills, and others. One of the grist-mills can grind 120 schepels [90 bushels] of meal in twenty-four hours, that is, five an hour. Returning to the house, we politely took our leave. Her residence is about a quarter of an hour from Albany up the river. . . .

Reprinted in: Kupperman, Karen Ordahl, ed. Major Problems in American Colonial History. Lexington, Mass.: C. C. Heath and Company, 1993, pp. 276–77.

Struggles to save estate

Maria van Rensselaer had to deal with significant business responsibilities and mounting debts. In addition, she had the task of obtaining a land grant that would guarantee family possession of the almost twenty-four square miles of the Rensselaerswyck property. Jeremias's younger brother, Nicholas, tried to take over the estate. Unlike many widows with young children, van Rensselaer did not remarry, so she did not have the help of a husband in fending off Nicholas's claim. When possible she relied on her father and her brother, Stephanus van Cortlandt, who lived in New York City. Eventually they reached a compromise whereby Nicholas was appointed director, van Rensselaer was elected treasurer, and Stephanus served as bookkeeper. When Nicholas died in 1678 his widow married Robert Livingston, a member of a prominent New York family. Livingston immediately tried to force division of Rensselaerswyck among various heirs. He continued his efforts until 1685, when he and the van Rensselaers agreed upon a settlement.

Manages Rensselaerswyck

During this time—in spite of her rapidly declining health—van Rensselaer remained in charge of the day-to-day running of the estate. She oversaw the leasing of farms to tenants. She also bought and sold land, wheat, and cattle, and maintained houses, barns, mills, and fences. In addition, "to keep up the dignity of the colony," she entertained distinguished visitors such as the governor. Her most important responsibility, however, was ensuring a future for her children. Since Jeremias had made no provisions for his family in his will, Maria sent Kiliaen to be apprenticed to (learn a trade from) a New York silversmith. Two of her other children went to New York City to live with her parents. All of the children eventually married well, and Kiliaen became the sole owner of Rensselaerswyck in 1687. When Maria died in 1689, at the age of forty-three, she had succeeded in securing for her children the most valuable estate in the colony. The van Rensselaers became an important family in early New York society.

For further research

The Correspondence of Jeremias Van Rensselaer, 1651–1674. Edited by A. J. F. Van Laer. Albany, N.Y.: University of the State of New York, 1932.

The Correspondence of Maria Van Rensselaer, 1669–1689. Edited by A. J. F. Van Laer. Albany, N.Y.: University of the State of New York, 1935.

James, Edward T., and others, eds. *Notable American Women,* Volume III. Cambridge, Mass.: Belknap Press of Harvard University Press, 1971, pp. 510–11.

Kupperman, Karen Ordahl, ed. *Major Problems in American Colonial History.* Lexington, Mass.: C. C. Heath and Company, 1993, pp. 276–77.

Giovanni da Verrazano

**1485
Tuscany, Italy
1528
Guadeloupe, West Indies**

**Italian explorer, first European
to sight eastern North America**

G iovanni da Verrazano (also Verrazzano) was an Italian explorer commissioned by the king of France to chart the eastern coast of North America, from Florida to Newfoundland. His main goal was to find a passage to Asia via the Pacific Ocean. Although Verrazano did not fulfill this mission, in 1524 he became the first European to sight New York Harbor as well as Narragansett Bay and other points along the northeastern Atlantic shore. Verrazano did not start any permanent settlements, yet he opened the way for Europeans who came to America in the early seventeenth century. For example, in 1624 the Dutch West India Company established New Amsterdam around New York Harbor and on Manhattan Island (see **Peter Stuyvesant** entry), and in 1636 English religious dissenter **Roger Williams** (see entry) founded Rhode Island on the mainland off Narragansett Bay. Verrazano also gave one of the earliest existing accounts of Native American life in North America. (The Viking explorer Erik the Red is credited with providing the first description of Native Americans when he discovered Greenland in 986.) The name Verrazano is familiar to North Americans today because of the Verrazano-Narrows Bridge, which connects Brooklyn to Staten Island.

" . . . we reached a new country, which had never before been seen by any one, either in ancient or modern times. . . . "

Giovanni da Verrazano.

Portrait: Giovanni da Verrazano.
Reproduced by permission of Corbis-Bettmann.

Sails to North America

Giovanni da Verrazano was born in 1485 into an aristocratic (ruling class) family in the Chianti region of Tuscany, Italy. Pursuing a career as a seaman, he moved in 1506 or 1507 to Dieppe, a port on the northwestern coast of France. From Dieppe he sailed to the eastern Mediterranean and may have traveled to Newfoundland in 1508. For the next fifteen years he worked his way up from seaman to navigator. In 1523 a group of Italian merchants in the French cities of Lyons and Rouen convinced the French king, François I, to sponsor Verrazano's voyage to North America. They hoped to find a more direct sea route to Asia, which was becoming a profitable trading partner for Europeans. Accompanied by his younger brother Girolamo, a mapmaker, Verrazano embarked from Dieppe in early 1524 on the ship *La Dauphine*. After crossing the Atlantic Ocean, Verrazano sighted land on March 1, 1524, at or near the site of present-day Cape Fear, North Carolina.

The Verrazano expedition sailed southward for a short distance and then turned back north. The ship landed near what is now Cape Hatteras on the Outer Banks, a sand bar separated from the mainland by Pamlico Sound. Unable to see the mainland from this vantage point, Verrazano assumed that the body of water on the other side of the sandbar was the Pacific Ocean. He concluded that he had found the route to China because Girolamo's maps incorrectly showed North America as a vast continent tapering to a narrow strip of land near the coast of North Carolina.

Discovers New York Harbor

Unable to find a passage through what he thought was an isthmus (a narrow strip of land connecting two large land areas), Verrazano sailed north along the coast, probably stopping at the present site of Kitty Hawk, North Carolina, where he encountered a group of Native Americans. He continued north but missed the entrance to both the Chesapeake and Delaware Bays. On April 17, however, Verrazano sailed into the upper reaches of present-day New York Harbor, which he described in his journal:

We found a very pleasant place, situated amongst certain little steep hills; from amidst which hills there ran down into the sea a great stream of water, which within the mouth was very deep, and from the

"the greatest delight on beholding us"

Following his expedition along the eastern coast of North America in 1524, Giovanni da Verrazano wrote a letter to King François I of France about his discoveries. The letter is considered an important document in the story of the exploration of North American. In his account Verrazano gave one of the earliest firsthand descriptions of Native peoples living in North America. The excerpt below describes his party's initial encounter with Native Americans, near Cape Fear, North Carolina.

Captain John de Verrazzano [Giovanni da Verrazano] to His Most Serene Majesty, the King of France, Writes:

[Around January 18, 1524] we reached a new country, which had never before been seen by any one, either in ancient or modern times. . . . we perceived, by the great fires near the coast, that it was inhabited . . . we drew in with the land and sent a boat on shore. Many people who were seen coming to the seaside fled at our approach, but occasionally stopping, they looked back upon us with astonishment, and some were at length induced, by various friendly signs, to come to us. These showed the greatest delight on beholding us, wondering at our dress, countenances and complexion. They then showed us by signs where we could more conveniently secure our boat, and offered us some of their provisions. That your Majesty may know all that we learned, while on shore, of their manners and customs of life, I will relate what we saw as

briefly as possible. They go entirely naked, except that about the loins they wear skins of small animals like martens [carnivorous animals related to the weasel] fastened with a girdle of plaited grass [a type of belt made with braided grass], to which they tie, all around the body, the tails of other animals hanging down to the knees; all other parts of the body and the head are naked. Some wear garments similar to birds' feathers.

The complexion of these people is black, not much different from that of the Ethiopians; their hair is black and thick, and not very long, it is worn tied back upon the head in the form of a little tail. In person they are of good proportions, of middle stature, a little above our own, broad across the breast, strong in arms, and well formed in the legs and other parts of the body; the only exception to their good looks is that they have broad faces, but not all, however, as we saw many that had sharp ones, with large black eyes and a fixed expression. They are not very strong in body, but acute in mind, active and swift of foot, as far as we could judge by observation. In these last two particulars they resemble the people of the east [Asia], especially those the most remote. We could not learn a great many particulars of their usages on account of our short stay among them, and the distance of ship from the shore. . . .

Reprinted in: Elliott, Emory, ed. American Literature: A Prentice Hall Anthology. *Englewood Cliffs, New Jersey: Prentice Hall, 1991, pp. 48–49.*

sea to the mouth of same, with the tide, which we found to rise 8 foot, any great vessel laden may pass up.

Verrazano was referring to the Hudson River, which was explored by **Henry Hudson** (see entry) in 1609.

Verrazano anchored *La Dauphine* at the narrows (entrance), which was later named in his honor. Leaving the harbor, he sailed up the coast to the entrance of Narragansett Bay. He found some islands in the bay and named one of them Rhode Island because it had the shape of Rhodes, the Greek island in the eastern Mediterranean. More than a hundred years later, **Roger Williams** (see entry) would take the name Rhode Island for the new English colony he founded on the mainland off Narragansett Bay. Verrazano then anchored his ship in present-day Newport Harbor, giving his crew a rest for two weeks. Exploring parties from the ship went as far inland as the site of Pawtucket. From Rhode Island, Verrazano led his expedition up the coast of Maine, proceeding north around Nova Scotia to Newfoundland before returning to Dieppe on July 8, 1524.

Meets death in West Indies

Immediately after landing in France, Verrazano wrote a report of his expedition for King François I. In his report he gave one of the earliest firsthand descriptions of the eastern coast of North America and the Native Americans who lived there. Verrazano's next expedition in 1527 was sponsored in part by Philippe de Chabot, admiral of France, because the king was preparing for war in Italy and could not spare any ships. On this trip Verrazano traveled to the coast of Brazil and brought back a valuable cargo of logwood for use in making textile dyes.

In 1528 Verrazano undertook another voyage to North America to renew his search for a passage to the Pacific, which he still thought could be found just south of Cape Fear. Leaving France in the spring of 1528, his party apparently reached the West Indies, where they followed the chain of islands northward. After landing at one of the islands, probably Guadeloupe, Verrazano was captured and killed by members of the hostile Carib tribe. His ships then sailed south to Brazil, where they obtained another cargo of logwood and returned to France.

For further research

Elliott, Emory, ed. *American Literature: A Prentice Hall Anthology.* Englewood Cliffs, N.J.: Prentice Hall, 1991, pp. 48–49.

"Giovanni Verrazano." http://www.greencastle.k12.in.us/stark/verrazano.htm Available July 13, 1999.

Morison, Samuel Eliot. *The Great Explorers: The European Discovery of America.* London, England: Oxford University Press, 1978.

Wroth, Lawrence C. *The Voyages of Giovanni da Verrazzano, 1524–1528.* New Haven, Conn.: Yale University Press, 1970.

George Whitefield

December 16, 1714
Gloucester, England
September 30, 1770
Newburyport, Massachusetts

Evangelical preacher and leader of the Great Awakening

"I drove 15 mad."

George Whitefield.

Portrait: George Whitefield.
Reproduced by permission of
Archive Photos, Inc.

George Whitefield (pronounced Whitfield) was an Anglican minister and leader of the early Methodist movement. Although he was ordained in the Anglican Church (also known as the Church of England, the official religion of the country), he preached Calvinist methodism to people of all Christian denominations in England, Scotland, Ireland, and America. (Calvinism is a religion that placed strong emphasis on the supreme power of God, the sinfulness of humankind, and the doctrine of predestination, which states that all human events are controlled by God.) Embarking on a series of evangelical revivals, he used improved transportation and a developing communications network to spread his message. In public he set aside his sweet and gentle personality to become a riveting, even intimidating speaker. Whitefield's dramatic preaching style electrified his audiences and sparked the American evangelical movement known as the Great Awakening.

One of the first public, religious figures to use the press (newspapers) to his own advantage, Whitefield published his journals, sermons, and letters. He directed his secretary to send press releases to newspapers, publicizing his tours and issuing favorable reports on his miraculous conversion of masses of people. Whitefield also inspired the publication of evangelical magazines, which sprang up throughout the colonies to praise his amazing successes. Eventually he became notorious for his abusiveness, and critics accused him of simply engaging in self-promotion. Nevertheless historians now recognize Whitefield as having made a significant impact on religion in the United States.

Leaves family business

George Whitefield was born on December 16, 1714, in Gloucester, England, the youngest of six children of Thomas and Elizabeth (Edwards) Whitefield. His parents were innkeepers in Gloucester, and upon Thomas's death in 1716 Elizabeth took over operation of the inn. In 1724, when Whitefield was ten, his mother married an iron seller named Longden. During his childhood Whitefield had the measles, which left him with crossed eyes and a squint. His mother wanted him to have a good education, so she sent him to St. Mary de Crypt school in Gloucester. He was a mediocre student but he excelled in drama, reportedly performing female roles in school productions. When he was fifteen he decided to leave St. Mary de Crypt, and for the next year and a half he worked at the inn as a "common drawer" (bartender). During this time one of Whitefield's brothers took over the family business. After a falling out with his brother's wife, Whitefield left the inn and went to Bristol, England. His mother then convinced him to apply to Oxford College.

Influenced by methodism

Whitefield was admitted to Oxford in 1732. He received financial assistance from Lady Elizabeth Hastings, who continued to support him and his causes later in life. At Oxford, Whitefield met John Wesley and Charles Wesley, brothers who had founded a society called the Oxford methodists in 1729. This Protestant Christian group earned the nickname "methodists" because of their emphasis on conducting their lives and religious study with "rule and method." They also advocated evangelical preaching (zealously encouraging believers and nonbelievers to make a personal commitment to Christianity). Methodists were highly critical of the

Anglican Church, which relied on priests and rituals as a means of communicating with God.

Before entering Oxford, Whitefield had heard about the Wesleys and had been intrigued by their ideas. He was not permitted to join their society until 1735, when he experienced a true religious conversion. Whitefield then returned to Gloucester and formed his own society. Upon his ordination as an Anglican deacon in July 1736, he preached his first sermon at St. Mary de Crypt. Departing from Anglican doctrine, he presented Methodist views of Christianity to his congregation with great emotion and enthusiasm. Amazed at the positive response from the audience, he reported, "I drove 15 mad." Whitefield had found his calling, and news of his remarkable speaking abilities reached churches in other cities. His popularity was further enhanced by the absence of the Wesleys, who had gone to spread the word of Methodism in America. When Whitefield gave his first sermon in London a month later, the audience initially ridiculed his youthful appearance, but soon were captivated by his dramatic flair. However, because of his emphasis on Methodism, Whitefield was not allowed to preach in Anglican churches.

Becomes celebrity preacher

In spite of being barred from the established church, Whitefield became an instant celebrity in England. Wherever he appeared, crowds seemed to materialize out of nowhere. He began delivering his sermons in the fields, an innovation that delighted his listeners. Being outdoors forced him to employ a more powerful voice and highly exaggerated gestures, which he then incorporated into his general preaching style. He also learned that by attacking the Anglican clergy for closing their pulpits to him, he could draw even larger crowds. A marvelous performer, he acted out his parts, used thunderstorms to punctuate his sentences, and created imaginary dialogues with biblical characters in tones that carried to the farthest edges of the crowd. He shouted, stomped, sang, and always wept. People regarded his cross-eyed stare as a sign of a supernatural presence that enabled him to keep one eye on heaven and the other on hell. Whitefield's message was simple: "Repent and you will be saved." He neither understood theology (religious philosophy) nor considered it to be important in his mission of inspiring people to seek salvation (forgiveness of sins).

Whitefield was offered a lucrative position in London, yet in spite of being in debt, he declined the opportunity. He planned instead to join the Wesleys in the Georgia colony, which was founded by **James Edward Oglethorpe** (see entry) in 1732. He delayed his departure, however, and engaged in missionary work in western England and London for eighteen months. During this time he had phenomenal success. In 1737 Whitefield's first published sermon was reprinted two times, and he was in constant demand as a speaker at charity events. He also raised funds for "the poor of Georgia," with the goal of starting a school and orphanage with the Wesleys. In order to carry out this plan, which would need support from English colonial officials, Whitefield knew he would have to become an Anglican minister. Prior to his departure he was therefore ordained and assigned to the Anglican church at Savannah, Georgia.

Goes to America

Whitefield went to America in 1739. When he arrived in Philadelphia, his reputation had preceded him. Philadelphians rushed to meet this "boy preacher" who had attained such fame before he was twenty-five years old. Whitefield toured Pennsylvania and New York, attracting large crowds and attacking the established clergy. Usually he preached outdoors or in dissenter churches. Whitefield then set out for the southern colonies, traveling through Maryland, Virginia, the Carolinas, and into Georgia. He continued to be greeted enthusiastically by huge crowds. When he reached Savannah he brought over 2,500 pounds (a sum of British money) that he had collected on preaching tours in the British Isles. The Wesleys had since departed for England after having problems with Georgia officials. With the money, Whitefield built an orphanage on 500 acres of land granted to him by Georgia trustees. He called the institution Bethesda. For the rest of his life he financially supported Bethesda, contributing large amounts of his own money.

Whitefield spent the winter in Georgia, but he composed press releases to insure that he was not forgotten in the other colonies. In April 1740 he returned to Philadelphia and even captivated American philosopher and scientist **Benjamin Franklin** (see entry) with his oratory. Whitefield was also

Benjamin Franklin supports Whitefield

Benjamin Franklin wrote this famous account of one of George Whitefield's sermons:

In 1739 arrived among us from England the Reverend Mr Whitefield who had made himself remarkable there as an itinerant [traveling] preacher. He was at first permitted to preach in some of our churches; but the clergy taking a disliking to him, soon refused him from their pulpits, and he was obliged to preach in the fields. The multitudes of all sects and denominations that attended his sermons were enormous, and it was a matter of speculation to me, who was one of the number, to observe the extraordinary influence of his oratory on his hearers, and how much they admired and respected him, not withstanding his common abuse of them, by assuring they were naturally "half beasts and half devils." It was wonderful to see the change soon made in the manners of our inhabitants, from being thoughtless or indifferent about religion, it seemed as if all the world were growing religious, so that one could not walk through the streets in an evening without hearing psalms sung in different families of every street. . . .

I happened soon after to attend one of his sermons, in the course of which I perceived he intended to finish with a collection and silently resolved he should get nothing from me. I had in my pocket a handful of copper money, three or four silver dollars, and five pistoles in gold. As he proceeded, I began to soften and concluded to give the coppers. Another stroke of his oratory made me ashamed of that and determined me to give the silver; and he finished so admirably that I emptied my pocket wholly into the collector's dish, gold and all. . . .

Some of Mr Whitefield's enemies affected to suppose that he would apply these collections to his own private emolument [gain], but I who was intimately acquainted with him (being employed in printing his sermons and journals, etc.) never had the least suspicion of his integrity, but am to this day decidedly of the opinion that he was in all his conduct a perfectly honest man.

Reprinted in: Middleton, Richard. Colonial America: A History, 1585–1776, second edition. Malden, MA: Blackwell Publishers, 1992, p. 290.

invited to Boston, Massachusetts, where he contributed to an intense debate between two Methodist factions, the liberals and the Calvinists. Whitefield took the Calvinist position, whereas John Wesley sided with the liberals (advocates of less strict interpretation of religious doctrine). As a consequence, followers of Whitefield became rivals of Wesley's supporters. (In 1741 Whitefield became the leader of the Calvinist Methodists.) While Whitefield was in Boston he also met **Jonathan Edwards** (see entry), the famous Puritan preacher.

Impressed by Whitefield's success in lifting Christians out of their "lethargy" (lack of religious fervor), Edwards invited the reformer to preach to his congregation at Northampton, Massachusetts. Whitefield then returned to Georgia for a well-publicized confrontation with an Anglican group, thus keeping his name in the news. In September he embarked on another tour of New England and then sailed to Scotland, where he sparked further revivals.

Power wanes

In 1741 Whitefield married Elizabeth Burnell James, a thirty-seven-year-old widow whom he met in Wales. Two years later the couple had their only child, a son, who died a few months after birth. Whitefield continued his missionary work, but by 1744 his meteoric rise to fame was coming to an end. Many other preachers also began delivering sermons outdoors. When Whitefield spoke, mobs gathered and managed to drown out his powerful voice. In an even more disturbing turn of events, former supporters either condemned his tactics or took them to extremes. For instance, Gilbert Tennent adopted Whitefield's strategy of attacking Anglican ministers, taking it to disturbing heights. Another well-known preacher, James Davenport, did a poor imitation of Whitefield's dramatic delivery. Worse yet, lay preachers (those who are not officially ordained) took up Whitefield's themes, proclaiming whatever views their audiences wanted to hear. As a result, churches splintered into bitter factions. Finally, the newspapers turned against Whitefield, running his opponents' unfavorable comments. Many critics blamed Whitefield for unleashing all of this disorder.

Repents for excesses

In 1745 an older, wiser, and more sober Whitefield returned to America. He apologized for his youthful egotism, which had caused religious chaos and unjustified abuse of other ministers. His heart had been in the right place, he maintained, and his dramatic flair had simply gotten out of hand.

Gilbert Tennent was a preacher who took some of George Whitefield's ideas to extreme measures. *Reproduced by permission of The Library of Congress.*

Whitefield continued his evangelical tours, but in a less confrontational manner. His revivals became routine and even acceptable to society. He spent more time in quiet and pious conversations with individuals rather than ranting in front of huge crowds. Whitefield also became involved in abolitionist (antislavery) efforts, and his final project was an effort to convert Bethesda orphanage into a college. The plan was never realized and the building burned in 1773. Whitefield preached his last sermon at Newburyport, Massachusetts, on September 29, 1770. He died the next day and, in accordance with his wishes, he was buried in Newburyport.

For further research

"George Whitefield." http://www.txdirect.net/_tgarner/webdoc5.htm Available July 13, 1999.

Lambert, Frank. *"Peddlar in Divinity": George Whitefield and the Transatlantic Revivals, 1737–1770.* Princeton, N.J.: Princeton University Press, 1994.

Middleton, Richard. *Colonial America: A History, 1585–1776,* second edition. Malden, Mass.: Blackwell Publishers, 1992, p. 290.

Pollock, John Charles. *George Whitefield and the Great Awakening.* Garden City, N.Y.: Doubleday, 1972.

Stout, Harry S. *The Divine Dramatist: George Whitefield and the Rise of Modern Evangelism.* Grand Rapids, Mich.: Eerdmans, 1991.

Roger Williams

c.1603
London, England
1683
Rhode Island

**Pioneer of religious freedom,
founder of Rhode Island**

Roger Williams was a religious leader whose spiritual journey forced him to leave one church and then another. He began his quest in 1636, five years after he arrived in the Massachusetts Bay Colony, when he became an enemy of the Puritans (those who advocated strict moral and spiritual codes). In the process he founded and governed Rhode Island, the first American colony to be based on separation of church and state. Unlike other colonists, Williams also believed that land in New England belonged to Native Americans and therefore should be purchased, rather than seized, by the British government. He is credited with starting the first Baptist church in America.

Shows intellectual abilities

Roger Williams was born around 1603 in London, England. He was the son of Alice and James Williams, a tailor. As a teenager he showed intelligence and motivation while he was in the employment of Edward Coke, a lawyer and influential figure in London. Williams's job was to record, in a type of shorthand, speeches and sermons that were delivered in the Star Chamber (court). Impressed with Williams's performance,

" . . . all men may walk as their consciences persuade them."

Roger Williams.

Portrait: Roger Williams.

Coke decided to finance his education at Sutton's Hospital, a school where Coke had placed only one other scholar. Williams proved to be a good student, and in 1623 Coke and others financed Williams's attendance at Cambridge University, where he continued to excel in his studies. At Cambridge Williams met **John Winthrop** (see entry), who later became governor of the Massachusetts Bay Colony.

After Williams graduated from Cambridge in 1626 he apparently was ordained as a clergyman in the Church of England (the official state religion; also called the Anglican Church). Records show that in 1629 he was serving as chaplain at the estate of William Masham in Essex. Evidence also indicates that Williams was offered a higher position in the church, but declined the appointment because he did not like the Anglican liturgy (religious service). Instead, he decided to move to Massachusetts to join Winthrop and other Puritans.

Rejects established church

Shortly before leaving England, Williams married Mary Warnard. The couple arrived in Massachusetts in 1631. Williams was invited to be an interim (temporary) pastor at a church in Boston, yet again he refused to serve. He objected that the congregation had not severed ties with the Church of England, which, as a branch of the British government, controlled religious activities in the colonies. Although New England ministers had been ordained in the Anglican Church, they held Puritan beliefs and were pursuing separation from Anglicanism. Nevertheless, Williams felt they were not sufficiently free of the English church. Therefore he and his wife settled in Salem, where he took an assignment as assistant teacher or minister.

One of Williams's first acts was to demand that Salem clergymen stop officiating at meetings (religious services) with the church congregation. He claimed that such a procedure interfered with the right of the individuals to interpret the Bible (the text that is the basis of Christianity). In addition, he forbade members of the church congregation to worship or pray with anyone, even family members, who had not undergone "regeneration." ("Regeneration" was the term for salvation, or forgiveness of sins directly from God. The Anglican Church required members to seek forgiveness through clergymen.) Soon Williams came into conflict with authorities in Boston because of his policies. He thought it best to leave Salem, so the Williamses went to Plymouth. In 1633, after their arrival at Plymouth, Mary Williams gave birth to their first child, a daughter.

Defends church-state separation

Within four months Williams had returned with his family to Salem. A year and a half later he was appointed chief teacher for the town. Magistrates (lawmakers) in Boston, the capital of the Massachusetts colony, immediately protested and called for Williams's removal. Yet the Salem congregation ignored the order, having already been well schooled by Williams on the rights of self-government. By this time Williams had been advocating the complete separation of church and state. He argued that religion was corrupted by any government interference in spiritual affairs. In his view, magistrates should have no power to use laws to enforce church doctrine (system of belief). Williams went even further by challenging the legal basis of the colony itself. He claimed that the English king, Charles I, had had no right to grant a charter (legal agreement) for the founding of Salem in 1629 because the land belonged to the Native Americans.

Massachusetts governor Winthrop and the colonial magistrates argued unsuccessfully with Williams until July 1635. At that time Williams was called before a council of judges at the general court in Boston to answer charges of holding "dangerous opinions." Specifically, officials were outraged by his statement that magistrates should not punish violation of church doctrines except in "such cases as did disturb the civil peace." This position severely undermined the authority of lawmakers, who presided over both the government and the church. The judges also required Williams to account for his equally threatening statement that "an unregenerated man" should not hold public office. According to Williams, anyone who had not achieved personal salvation— that is, gained forgiveness of sins directly from God and not through a clergyman—was not a "true" Christian. Therefore, Williams was implying that many current government officials were not true Christians.

Roger Williams's departure from Salem. *Reproduced by permission of Corbis-Bettmann.*

Banned from Massachusetts

Williams refused to reject any of his "dangerous opinions." At first the Salem congregation supported him against the Boston council. Gradually, however, Williams's followers feared being banished from (sent away and forbidden to return) the colony or ostracized (treated as outsiders) within the Salem community. On October 9, after four months of resisting pressure from the judges to change his views, Williams was banished from Massachusetts. The judges initially decreed that he must leave within six weeks, but they later relented and let him remain in Salem until spring. In the meantime, Williams was not allowed to "go about to draw others to his opinions." The council even offered to withdraw the sentence of banishment if Williams agreed to cease spreading his disruptive views. To the contrary, he ignored the council's verdict altogether and proceeded to hold meetings in his home.

In January 1636 the council called Williams back to Boston. When he refused to go the judges sent a boat to Salem, giving the captain orders to place Williams under arrest and put him on a ship to England. In the meantime, Winthrop had warned Williams about the council's plans. Winthrop advised him to flee south into Native American territory, which was outside English jurisdiction. Accompanied by four or five companions, Williams left his family behind and departed Salem in the middle of winter. He later wrote that he and the other men trekked the wilderness in bitter weather for fourteen weeks, "not knowing what bread or bed did mean." Williams and his party finally reached the region ruled by **Massasoit** (see entry), chief of the Wampanoag tribe, who gave them food and shelter. Williams and Massasoit reportedly became close friends, and Massasoit probably influenced Williams's understanding of Native American culture and his advocacy of their land rights. The Wampanoags sold Williams a tract of land on the Seekonk River near the Plymouth colony, where he had once lived. In April he began making preparations for a settlement. Then **William Bradford** (see entry), governor of Plymouth and a friend of Williams, pointed out that Williams had claimed some land that already belonged to the Plymouth colony.

Founds colony on religious freedom

The following month Williams and his friends crossed the river and started a settlement called Providence. They were later joined by Williams's wife and two children. Williams was sure to evenly distribute land to insure economic equality and institute a "democratical" government, under which "all men may walk as their consciences persuade them." Any additional land for the settlement was to be purchased from Native Americans. In 1638 the Native Americans granted the Providence settlers more land alongside Plymouth.

As soon as Williams founded the Providence colony it became a refuge for dissenters (protesters) from Massachusetts and England. Some were seeking the right to worship in their own churches, while others were drawn to a more unconventional view of Christianity. Among them was **Anne Hutchinson** (see entry), who was banished from Massachusetts in March 1638. She joined her husband on Aquidneck Island, which had been bought by Puritan exiles, on Narragansett Bay near Williams's settlement. Hutchinson was followed by more than eighty families of her supporters who had also been excommunicated (expelled) from the Puritan church. One of the most prominent was **Mary Dyer** (see entry), a Quaker dissenter who was executed for heresy (holding beliefs that violate church doctrine) in Boston two decades later. ("Quaker" is a commonly used term for the Religious Society of Friends, who believe an individual is endowed with an "inner light" that makes possible direct communication with the Holy Spirit. Quakers do not ordain clergymen or observe formal worship services.)

Starts first Baptist church

In 1639 Williams organized the first Baptist church in North America. He had long been intrigued by the views of the Anabaptists (a name later shortened to Baptists), a Christian group who believed that infants should not be baptized (a ceremony that involves being inducted into the Christian faith through immersion in water). According to Anabaptists, baptism should be administered only to adults who have accepted church doctrines. In keeping with these views, Williams became a Baptist and his friends baptized each other. Later Williams condemned adult baptism because it was not administered by an apostle (a founder of the faith) as the Scriptures specified. Then he began to have doubts about whether other members of the church had actually achieved salvation, finally reaching the conclusion that he could take communion only with his wife. (Communion is a rite involving the consumption of bread and wine, which represent the body and blood of Jesus Christ, the founder of Christianity.) These same doubts eventually drove Williams to the opposite extreme, and he administered baptism and communion to anyone, since no human can be certain who has gained salvation. Finally Williams left the ministry entirely, contending that the Scriptures do not mention an organized church or official clergy. Although he remained a Christian, he considered himself a "Seeker" (one who rejects formal church doctrine without leaving the Christian faith).

Charters Rhode Island

By 1643 Williams's colony had grown to four settlements—Providence, Portsmouth, Warwick, and Newport—on Narragansett Bay. In 1644 Williams made a trip to England and secured a charter for a self-governing colony called Rhode

Island, a name he chose because Aquidneck Island reminded him of the Greek island of Rhodes. After challenges to the legality of the charter in 1651, Williams served as president from 1654 to 1657 in order to guarantee the continuance of political and religious freedoms. During the first year of his presidency Jews settled in Newport, then Quakers followed in large numbers. Williams's own tolerance was eventually tested by the Quakers because they seemed to ignore the Bible and Christ in favor of the "inner light" possessed by all Christians. When George Fox, the founder of the Religious Society of Friends, visited Newport in 1672, Williams was determined to confront him in a debate. Now over seventy years old, Williams dragged his frail body into a boat and rowed alone the thirty miles to meet Fox. The Quaker leader had already departed, so Williams engaged Fox's associates in a battle of published words.

Sees Native American decline

In 1675 Williams's longstanding friendship with the Native Americans was also severely tested. That same year Massasoit's son and successor, **Metacom** (see entry), initiated a conflict popularly known as King Philip's War (Metacom was called King Philip by the English). Metacom was seeking revenge for the execution of three Wampanoag warriors by Plymouth colonists, who had charged them with murdering an Englishman. Williams was unable to stop the war and, at the age of seventy-three, he was pressed into service as a captain of militia (colonists' army). After eighteen months the Wampanoags were completely defeated, with casualties totaling three thousand—five times the number of colonist deaths. Thus began the breakdown of trust between colonists and Native Americans that Williams had cultivated for nearly four decades.

Williams died in 1683 at the age of eighty-one. During his lifetime he had been a prolific writer. One of his earliest publications was *Key into the Language of America* (1643), a book on the Narragansett language. He is best known today for *The Bloudy Tenent of Persecution for Cause of Conscience* (1644), in which he stated his religious and political views. Williams was reportedly a charming and honorable man who was admired by everyone who knew him, including Puritans who did not agree with his free-thinking views.

For further research

Gaustad, Edwin S. *Liberty of Conscience: Roger Williams in America.* Grand Rapids, Mich.: Eerdmans, 1991.

Miller, Perry. *Roger Williams: His Contribution to the American Tradition.* New York: Atheneum, 1962.

Roger Williams National Memorial. http://www.nps.gov/rowi/ Available July 13, 1999.

Winslow, Ola. *Master Roger Williams.* New York: Macmillan, 1957.

John Winthrop
1588
Suffolk, England
1649
Massachusetts

Puritan leader, first governor of Massachusetts Bay Colony

John Winthrop was a stern Puritan (member of a Christian group that held strict moral and spiritual views) and the first governor of the Massachusetts Bay Colony. Prior to emigrating (moving from one country to another) to America, he led a comfortable life as a wealthy lawyer and landowner in England. Then in the 1620s the country became embroiled in religious, economic, and political turmoil. Times were especially difficult for Puritans, who pressed for reforms in the Anglican Church (the official religion; also known as the Church of England) and took a dim view of the moral climate of England. Consequently, they were deprived of political rights, such as serving in Parliament (the British legislative body). Their religious practices were suppressed and held up to ridicule. Winthrop was among the thousands of Puritans who decided to leave their homeland for a place that would allow them religious and political freedom. Leading the Massachusetts Bay Company, Winthrop arrived in Massachusetts in 1630. Although he was an autocratic (dictatorial) governor, he made significant contributions to the survival of the young colony for nearly two decades. His book *The History of New England from 1630 to 1649* remains a valuable resource for scholars.

" . . . the eies of all people are uppon us. . . . "

John Winthrop.

Portrait: John Winthrop.
Reproduced by permission of The Library of Congress.

Born to life of privilege

John Winthrop was born in 1588 in Suffolk, England, into a life of privilege as a member of the English gentry. His father, Adam Winthrop, was trained as a lawyer and was a shrewd businessman. After inheriting an estate called Groton Manor from his own father, Adam rented and bought land in the area, growing cash crops that he sold in nearby London. Adam's second wife, John's mother, was Anne Browne, the daughter of a wealthy merchant. As the couple's only son, John would one day inherit the manor at Groton.

In keeping with his station in life Winthrop received a good education. During his early years his teacher was a local minister, who prepared Winthrop for Cambridge University, the college his father had attended. In 1603, at the age of four-teen, Winthrop entered Cambridge. Although he left within two years without a degree, he was following the custom of most young gentlemen of the time. Winthrop also briefly attended Gray's Inn, one of the famed Inns of Court where the elite studied law. Again he left without a degree. College had apparently been an unpleasant experience, as he later wrote: "For being there neglected, and despised, I went up and down mourning with myself."

Marries early

Winthrop returned to Groton Manor in 1605, at the age of seventeen. By that time he had also become a Puritan. Immediately he entered into an arranged and advantageous marriage to Mary Forth of Great Stambridge, Essex. Again he was doing what was expected of a man of his social rank. The following year the Winthrops had a son, John Jr., and over the next decade they had five more children. Six months after Mary died in 1615, John wed Thomasine Clopton. Yet this marriage lasted only a year because Thomasine also died. Winthrop married for a third time in 1618, when he was thirty years old. His new wife, Margaret Tyndal, shared his religious convictions, and they lived happily together for nearly thirty years.

By 1617 Winthrop had inherited Groton Manor. While serving as a justice of the peace, he began to study law more seriously. Legal knowledge was essential to his duties as lord of Groton Manor, which included presiding over court for his

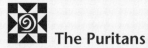

The Puritans

The Puritan movement began around 1560, during the reign of Queen Elizabeth I. Pressing for reform of the Church of England, many Protestants claimed that Elizabeth had allowed the Church to remain too much like the Roman Catholic Church. They believed the Scriptures (books that make up the Bible) did not allow for the appointment of bishops, who wore elaborate robes and conducted complex rituals. They also believed in predestination (the doctrine that all events are destined by God) and argued that the Bible did not permit the establishment of a state church. Setting out to purify the Church of England, they dressed simply and observed strict moral and religious codes—thus earning the name "Puritans." At first the Puritans had no intention of separating from the Anglican Church, hoping to change it from within, but gradually small groups began holding private worship services. Early Puritans followed the doctrines of French Protestant theologian John Calvin, organizing their church into parishes in which members elected their own ministers. Soon the major Puritan denomination was the Presbyterian Church, which had a central government. Other denominations were the Separatists and Congregationalists, who differed from the Presbyterians in regarding a single congregation as a church in its own right. The Separatists and Congregationalists also asserted that people could interpret the Scriptures on their own, without the aid of a clergyman or a formal worship service. During the reigns of King James I and King Charles I the Puritans experienced intense persecution. This led them to flee England in search of religious and political freedom in other European countries and in America.

tenants. After he and Margaret were married, they lived first at Groton and then on lands in Essex that she had contributed as a dowry (the money or land brought by a bride to her husband at marriage). At both places Winthrop gained extensive experience in managing large estates. Thus he had embarked on a life as a country squire (gentleman) when events took him in an entirely unexpected direction.

Encounters hard times

During the 1620s England was embroiled in religious and economic turmoil. The religious conflicts began in 1534 when King Henry VIII broke with the Roman Catholic Church and formed the Church of England as the official religion in England. English Protestants continued to press for church reforms. Henry's daughter, Queen Elizabeth I, upheld his policies and the Puritan movement originated during her reign. The Puritans claimed the Church of England was as corrupt and excessive as the Catholic Church. Elizabeth's successor, King James I, disliked Puritans, seeing them as a threat to the church and to the Crown (monarchy or royal family). The Puritans predicted the moral and economic ruination of England. Economic problems seemed to bear out their dire warnings when the textile (cloth) industry, the basis of the English economy, went into a decline that rippled through the entire country. Suffolk, the county where Groton Manor was located, was hit especially hard. As a result, Winthrop's financial situation became bleak. To make matters worse his family was growing. Four of his six children from his first marriage had survived, and he had three sons from his third marriage. (Eventually Winthrop fathered sixteen children.)

In 1627, through connections in the royal government, Winthrop obtained a position as an attorney in His Majesty's Court of Wards and Liveries. The court controlled the estates of orphaned children until they came of legal age. This job took Winthrop away from his wife and family, but enabled him to witness governmental corruption firsthand. In 1625 King Charles I, son of James I, ascended the English throne. Charles was not only more rigid and less tolerant of Puritans, but he also was married to a Roman Catholic, which was a source of great anxiety for Puritans. Charles accepted a new direction for the Church of England that promoted good works as a means of salvation (forgiveness of sins). In other words, Church members would perform good deeds and clergymen would then forgive their sins. Puritans were horrified at this development, since they believed only God could determine who had earned salvation. Consequently, many Puritans left England for European countries such as the Netherlands. Others, including Winthrop, looked toward America.

Leads Massachusetts Bay Company

In 1629 Winthrop joined the New England Company. The previous year the Council for New England (a private organization that promoted trade and settlement in New England) had granted the company a parcel of land between the Charles and Merrimack Rivers in Massachusetts. One of the negotiators of the patent (title or deed) was **John Endecott** (see entry), who was then living in Massachusetts. In 1629 the New England Company received a royal charter (a right to land granted by the king) under the new name of "Governor and Company of the Massachusetts Bay in New England." It became known as the Massachusetts Bay Company. Although the group had initially planned to promote trade in the colony, their emphasis soon shifted to religion. Winthrop and other Puritans saw the venture as an ideal opportunity to start a settlement in which they could enjoy religious and political freedom.

In 1629 a group led by Winthrop signed the Cambridge Agreement. The document stated that, once the group reached America, they could buy out the company and take over the charter and government of the colony. Thus the Massachusetts Bay Company was the only colonizing venture that did not come under the control of governors in England. In August 1629 Winthrop pledged to move his whole family to Massachusetts. In October, when he was chosen head of the company, he organized the fleet that would take them to America. To help meet expenses he sold Groton Manor. After arranging for his family to join him in 1631, he and the first Massachusetts Bay settlers set out on the ship *Arbella*. During the voyage Winthrop delivered one of the most famous sermons in American history, "A Modell of Christian Charity." In his speech he compared the Puritans' new enterprise to "a Citty upon a Hill," and he warned that the eyes of the world were upon them. For Winthrop the trip to America was a holy mission, a vision that helped him lead the settlers through subsequent hard times. Yet his sense of divine purpose also made him a fanatic who lost sight of human needs and tolerated few opinions that did not conform to his own.

Named first governor

The *Arbella* arrived at Salem, Massachusetts, in 1630. Shortly thereafter, Winthrop founded a settlement on the Shawmut peninsula. As head of the Massachusetts Bay Company he took over leadership of the colony from Endecott and became governor. Winthrop held the position for four years (he

Winthrop's "Citty upon a Hill"

In 1631 John Winthrop sailed with the Puritans, the first Massachusetts Bay Colony settlers, aboard the ship *Arbella*. During the voyage he delivered one of the most famous sermons in American history, "A Modell of Christian Charity." Near the end of his sermon Winthrop likened the Puritans' new enterprise to "a Citty upon a Hill," with the eyes of the world upon them:

> . . . the Lord will be our God and delight to dwell among us, as his owne people and will commaund a blessing upon us in all our wayes, soe that wee shall see much more of his wisdome power goodnes and truthe then formerly wee have beene acquainted with, wee shall finde that the God of Israell is among us, when tenn of us shall be able to resist a thousand of our enemies, when hee shall make us a prayse and glory, that men shall say of succeeding plantacions: the lord make it like that of New England: for wee must Consider that wee shall be as a Citty upon a Hill, the eies of all people are uppon us; soe that if wee shall deale falsely with our god in this worke wee have undertaken and soe cause him to withdrawe his present help from us, wee shall be made a story and a by-word through the world, wee shall open the mouthes of enemies to speake evill of the wayes of god and all professours for Gods sake. . . .

Reprinted in: Gunn, Giles, ed. Early American Writing. *New York: Penguin Books, 1994, p. 112.*

was eventually elected governor twelve times). The first order of business was to organize the colony on the basis of religious congregations (known as congregationalism), whereby each congregation could establish itself and choose its own minister. This decision was later blamed for unwanted religious diversity. Winthrop also established the colony's government, keeping power in his own hands with the aid of a few assistants. He gave little authority to men called freemen, who served on a general assembly. In 1634, when the freemen challenged Winthrop to show them the company's charter, they realized they were entitled to more power than he had allowed them. The freedmen then formed a representative assembly, elected members from each town, and voted Winthrop out of office.

During the next three years Massachusetts was torn apart by religious dissension. In 1637 the colony turned to Winthrop and elected him governor again. Winthrop's political fortunes over the next several years reflected the chaos in the colony. In 1640 he was replaced as governor, only to be reelected in 1642. After serving for two terms he was demoted to deputy-governor for a year. During this time Winthrop adhered to strict theocratic principles (rule of the church by the government) and bitterly opposed the activities of religious dissidents (those who question church doctrines). Among the most troublesome were **Roger Williams** and **Anne Hutchinson** (see separate entries), whom Winthrop was instrumental in banning from the Massachusetts Bay Colony.

Finally, in 1646, Winthrop was elected governor again. When his wife Margaret died in 1647, he married a fourth time, to Martha Coytmore. Within a year she bore him a son, his sixteenth child. Winthrop was still serving as governor when he died in 1649 at the age of sixty-eight. Although the colony had survived under his leadership, Massachusetts soon outgrew the narrow authoritarianism that had been useful to him during the first years of its founding. Winthrop made a lasting contribution to American history with his journal, which was published as *The History of New England from 1630 to 1649* in 1908.

For further research

Dunn, Richard S. *Puritans and Yankees: The Winthrop Dynasty of New England 1630–1717*. Princeton, N.J.: Princeton University Press, 1962.

Gunn, Giles, ed. *Early American Writing*. New York: Penguin Books, 1994, p. 112.

"John Winthrop" in *The Puritans: American Literature Colonial Period (1608-1700)*. http://www.falcon.jmu.edu/-ramseyil/amicol.htm Available July 13, 1999.

Morgan, Edward S. *The Puritan Dilemma: The Story of John Winthrop*. Boston: Little, Brown, 1958.

John Woolman

October 19, 1720
Ancocas, New Jersey
October 7, 1772
York, England

Quaker minister and abolitionist

John Woolman was a Quaker minister who led a campaign against slavery. (See box for description of Quakers.) His efforts required considerable courage because there was no organized abolition movement (the group that wanted to outlaw slavery) during the early eighteenth century and there was much resistance to his beliefs at the time. By the late 1700s, after Woolman's death, however, Quakers had prohibited slave-holding within the Religious Society of Friends (the official name of their group). They then emerged as leaders in the abolition movement. Woolman was also an essayist who kept a detailed journal. Although he was relatively unknown outside the Quaker community during his lifetime, his *Journal* has since become an American literary classic.

Becomes Quaker minister

John Woolman was born on October 19, 1720, in Ancocas, New Jersey, the son of Samuel Woolman, a Quaker farmer. The name of his mother is not known. There is little information about Woolman's early life, although records

Portrait: John Woolman.
Reproduced by permission of
The Granger Collection Ltd.

The Quakers

Quakers are members of the Religious Society of Friends (also called the Friends Church), a Christian group that was originally affiliated with the English Puritans (see box in **John Winthrop** entry). The Quaker movement arose in England during the mid-seventeenth century. At first "Quaker" was a term of ridicule, but eventually they adopted the name themselves. The founder of Quakerism was English religious leader George Fox, who stressed reliance on the teachings of Jesus of Nazareth (Christ) as a guide to living one's life. Fox advocated abandoning all ritual and clergy, contending that church buildings, formal worship services, and ordained ministers were not necessary. Therefore the early Quakers gathered informally in small, plain meeting houses, with men and women seated on opposite sides of the room. They sat in silence, waiting for an "inner light," or word from God, to come to them. Any man or woman who felt inspired by God could stand and speak to the group. Over time, members who showed a special talent for speaking were recorded as ministers. As Quakerism spread rapidly throughout England, Scotland, and Ireland, the Friends were subjected to violent persecution because they were viewed as a threat to other established religions. Consequently they sought refuge on the continent of Europe, in the American colonies, and the West Indies.

show that he worked on his parents' farm until he was twenty-one. He then settled in the nearby town of Mount Holly, where he operated a shop (possibly a bakery) for about two years. In 1743, after his business became successful, he began working as a tailor and earned extra money by keeping an orchard. He lived in the simple manner of the Quakers, wearing undyed garments and buying only the basic necessities. In 1743 Woolman also set out on his first excursion as a Quaker minister, traveling—often on foot—from New England to the Carolinas to attend yearly Quaker meetings. During his lifetime he made nearly thirty of these trips, and he conducted his ministry without receiving any pay. By 1749 he was married to Sarah Ellis, with whom he had several children.

Slaves held in all colonies

Soon after Woolman started his travels he became concerned about serious social issues of the day, particularly the mistreatment of slaves. By the mid-eighteenth century, African slaves had been held in the colonies for over 125 years, having been introduced into British settlements in Virginia in 1619. During the previous century Spanish and Portuguese plantation owners in the West Indies had found that Africans were better workers than Native Americans, who resisted enslavement. Soon African slaves were essential to the American plantation economy and the slave trade became a booming business. The slave-trade route formed a triangle: ships loaded with European-made goods departed from British ports and landed on the west coast of Africa, where the goods would be exchanged for slaves. Then the slaves were transported to the American colonies or the West Indies and traded for agricultural products (see **Olaudah Equiano** entry). Finally, completing the triangle, the ships took this cargo back to England.

At first Africans in North America were able to buy their freedom and own land, and owners made an effort to keep slave families together (see **Anthony Johnson** entry). But gradually Africans lost these rights and, as slaves were routinely bought and sold, families were broken apart. By the 1740s, when Woolman was making his journey through the colonies, the majority of African slaves remained in bondage throughout their lives. They worked mainly on plantations in southern colonies, but they also were being held as household servants and laborers in all of the colonies, in both the South and the North. Slaves were worth large sums of money, so harsh laws gave owners the right to demand the return of runaways, who were considered legal "property."

Protests slavery

Especially disturbing to Woolman was the fact that Africans were being held as slaves by Christians, and even by Quakers. In fact, in the 1720s, the Society of Friends had expelled at least one member who opposed the keeping of slaves. Woolman therefore resolved to mount a vigorous abolitionist campaign. When he traveled southward along the eastern seaboard, he carried his message to slave holders. In

from *Considerations on the Keeping of Negroes*

In 1743 John Woolman began making trips to yearly Quaker meetings in colonies from New England to the Carolinas. During his visits he became alarmed at the mistreatment of African slaves. Woolman then vowed to wage an abolitionist campaign, which involved writing essays as well as making personal contacts with slave owners and traders. One of his most famous essays is *Considerations on the Keeping of Negroes* (1754). In the excerpt below Woolman sets out the moral argument against the holding of slaves.

> There are various Circumstances amongst them that keep Negroes, and different Ways by which they fall under their Care; and, I doubt not, there are many well disposed Persons amongst them who desire rather to manage wisely and justly in this difficult Matter, than to make Gain of it.
>
> But the general Disadvantage which these poor Africans lie under in an enlight'ned Christian Country, having often fill'd me with real Sadness, and been like undigested Matter on my Mind, I now think it my Duty, through Divine Aid, to offer some Thoughts thereon to the Consideration of others.
>
> When we remember that all Nations are of one Blood. . . . [a passage from the Old Testament of the Bible] that in this World we are but Sojourners [temporary residents], that we are subject to the like Afflictions [sufferings] and Infirmities [diseases] of Body, the like Disorders and Frailties [weaknesses] in Mind, the like Temptations, the same Death, and the same Judgement, and, that the Alwise Being is Judge and Lord over us all, it seems to raise an Idea of a general Brotherhood, and a Disposition easy to be touched with a Feeling of each others Afflictions: But when we forget those Things, and look chiefly at our outward Circumstances, in this and some Ages past, constantly retaining in our Minds the Distinction betwixt [between] us and them, with respect to our Knowledge and Improvement in Things divine, natural and artificial, our Breasts being apt to be filled with fond Notions of Superiority, there is Danger of erring [making mistakes] in our Conduct toward them.

Reprinted in: Gunn, Giles, ed. Early American Writing. New York: Penguin Books, 1994, p. 391.

Rhode Island he tried to persuade shipowners not to transport slaves from Africa to North America. He refused to buy any products connected with the slave trade, and he would not accept hospitality from slave owners. Frequently he made payment for lodging directly to slaves themselves. Deciding to limit his abolitionist efforts within the Quaker community, he encountered continuing resistance. Yet Woolman was persistent, never wavering from his convictions.

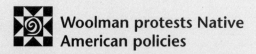

Woolman protests Native American policies

As John Woolman traveled through the American colonies, he became alarmed at policies toward Native Americans. For instance, while visiting the Pennsylvania frontier he learned that settlers were getting Native Americans drunk on rum, then tricking them into signing treaties that gave up huge tracts of land. Woolman therefore pressed for prohibitions against selling rum to Native Americans and he supported better policies for acquiring land.

Writes on injustice

While trying to convince other Quakers to oppose slavery, Woolman wrote essays on social injustices. The essays were printed in publications for Quaker readers. In addition to addressing the evils of slave holding, Woolman extended his compassion to Native Americans, poor settlers, and even mistreated farm animals. He contended that political and social problems could be solved only through spiritual efforts. In accordance with his Quaker beliefs, he wrote that people must live simply and show concern for their fellow human beings. At the age of thirty-six Woolman began keeping a journal in which he examined the state of his own soul. He made regular entries in the journal until his death sixteen years later.

Succeeds in abolition efforts

Woolman's abolitionist activities eventually produced results. He persuaded Quaker communities to make public protests against slavery, and he convinced owners to free their slaves. He was joined by others who shared his views, and in 1760, Quakers in New England, New York, and Pennsylvania ceased the buying and selling of slaves. The Society of Friends was then at the forefront of the antislavery movement. In 1772 Woolman went to London, England, to attend the annual meeting of Quaker ministers and elders. At first the English Quakers thought he looked peculiar in his colorless clothes, but he soon formed friendships with his fellow Friends. After the conference he left London to visit communities in the outlying English counties. In late September, after reaching York, Woolman was stricken with smallpox (at that time a fatal epidemic disease). A little more than a week later he died at the home of Thomas Priestman.

Journal becomes classic

Woolman was relatively unknown outside Quaker circles during his lifetime. Upon the publication of *The Journal of*

John Woolman in 1775, however, he became an important social critic and literary figure. Over the next century the journal was reprinted at least ten times and some of his essays were translated into German and French. Prominent nineteenth-century American and British thinkers praised Woolman's work for its simple style as well its moving expression of the Quaker soul. Several American writers were directly influenced by his views. Modern scholars rank Woolman's *Journal* along with the *Autobiography* of **Benjamin Franklin** (see entry) as one of the great classics of American personal narrative. Woolman is now known as the "Quaker saint," and his *Journal* remains in print today. Several selections from the work have been included in texts for high-school and college students.

For further research

Cady, Edwin Harrison. *John Woolman.* New York: Washington Square Press, 1965.

Dalglish, Doris N. *People Called Quakers.* Freeport, N.Y.: Books for Libraries Press, 1969.

Gunn, Giles, ed. *Early American Writing.* New York: Penguin Books, 1994, p. 391.

John Peter Zenger

1697
Germany
July 28, 1746
New York, New York

Printer and journalist, pioneer of freedom of the press

John Peter Zenger was a German-born printer and journalist who published the *New-York Weekly Journal*. The newspaper was a political forum for colonists who opposed the policies of New York governor William Cosby. Although Zenger did not write the articles he published, he was responsible for their content. Charged with libel (making a false statement that exposes another person to public contempt) in 1734, he was arrested and held in jail for ten months. After he finally went to trial his lawyer, Andrew Hamilton, won an acquittal (not-guilty verdict) that established the first victory for freedom of the press (the right of newspapers to print truthful information) in the American colonies.

Apprenticed to prominent printer

John Peter Zenger was born in Germany in 1697. At age thirteen he sailed to the New York colony with his parents, brother, and sister. His father (whose name is not known) died during the voyage, leaving Zenger's mother, Johanna, to care for the family. In 1711 Zenger went to work as an apprentice (one who learns an art or trade in exchange for doing work) with printing pioneer William Bradford (see box). When Zenger completed his apprenticeship in 1719 he married Mary White, who died a short time later. In 1720 he relocated to Chestertown, Maryland, where he was granted the authority to print the session laws (laws passed during official meetings) of the Maryland Assembly (legislative body). Within two years Zenger had returned to New York. In 1722 he married Anna Catherine Maulin, and the next year he became a freeman (one who has full rights of a citizen) of the city. After a brief partnership with Bradford, Zenger started his own business in 1726. Over the next seven years he printed mainly political and religious pamphlets, which were written in the Dutch language. In 1730 he printed *Arithmetica* by Peter Venema, the first arithmetic text published in New York.

Prints controversial newspaper

The turning point in Zenger's life occurred in 1733, when he was appointed editor of the *New-York Weekly Journal,* a new political paper. Earlier, Cosby had angered New York residents by dismissing Lewis Morris as chief justice (principal judge of the colonial court) and replacing him with James De Lancey, a Cosby ally. The *Journal* was started by lawyers, merchants, and other citizens who thought Cosby had misused his powers as governor. New York was a royal colony—that is, it was controlled by the British monarchy, which appointed the governor. (Founded by Dutch proprietor **Peter Stuyvesant** [see entry] in 1645, New York was taken over by the English in 1664.) Staging a revolt, they organized the newspaper as a forum for their opinions. Upon taking the position with the *Journal,* Zenger found himself in opposition to his former mentor, Bradford, who published the progovernment *New York Gazette,* the first newspaper in New York.

 William Bradford

In 1711 John Peter Zenger went to work as an apprentice for American printing pioneer William Bradford (1663–1752; not to be confused with William Bradford, founder of Plymouth, Massachusetts). Bradford began his career in Philadelphia, Pennsylvania, where he started the first printing press as well as the first paper mill in the American colonies. Bradford was also the defendant in the first court case involving freedom of the press in the United States. In the early 1690s he was arrested for printing a pamphlet that was critical of the Quaker government in the Pennsylvania colony. Bradford was put on trial but no verdict was reached. The not-guilty verdict in the Zenger trial in 1735 is therefore considered the first significant victory for freedom of the press in America.

Andrew Hamilton

Andrew Hamilton (1676?–1741) was a prominent colonial American lawyer. Born in Scotland, he emigrated to Maryland, where he practiced law. He then moved to Pennsylvania, becoming attorney general in 1717. Hamilton was brought into the Zenger libel case in New York after all of Zenger's lawyers were disbarred by the administration of Governor William Cosby. As publisher of the antigovernment newspaper *New-York Weekly Journal,* Zenger had been jailed and charged with printing false statements about Cosby. Hamilton presented a brilliant defense of Zenger, winning a not-guilty verdict from the jury and thus establishing truth as a defense against charges of libel.

Charged with libel

The first issue of the *Journal* appeared on November 5, 1733. Since Zenger had not fully mastered the English language, he did not write any major articles. Most of the pieces, which accused Cosby of governing without the will of the people, were probably written by the backers of the newspaper. Yet Zenger as publisher was responsible for every word. After the *Journal* had been running for nearly a year, the New York council (law-making body) decided to punish Zenger. They ordered the burning of four especially offensive issues of the *Journal.* Court officials refused to carry out the order, however, and the sheriff's African slave finally burned the papers. Zenger was arrested within a few days and his bail (payment for freedom from imprisonment before a trial) was set at four hundred pounds (a sum of British money), plus two hundred pounds in bail insurance. He could not raise the funds, so he was sent to prison. For several days he was held in isolation, then he spent almost ten months behind bars. During this time Anna Zenger published the newspaper each week, smuggling her husband's instructions out of the prison.

Freedom of press established

Zenger was brought to trial for criminal libel in April 1735. His attorneys immediately challenged the appointment of the politically powerful Chief Justice De Lancey, who was obviously loyal to Cosby, to preside over the trial. The Cosby administration then disbarred (expelled from the legal profession) Zenger's attorneys and the case was delayed until August. By this time Zenger was being represented by Andrew Hamilton, a Philadelphia attorney and the most prominent lawyer in the American colonies. Presenting the case for the New York

The trial of John Peter Zenger

In 1736 Andrew Hamilton wrote a word-for-word account of the trial (under Zenger's name) in which he was accused of publishing libelous statements against the governor of New York, William Cosby. The following excerpts from Zenger's report represent the views of the major figures in the trial: New York attorney general Richard Bradley argued the government's case against Zenger; Andrew Hamilton was the lawyer who successfully defended Zenger; and Chief Justice James De Lancey, the presiding judge and a Cosby ally, attempted to prevent jury members from reaching their own verdict.

Attorney General Bradley: . . . The case before the Court is, whether Mr. Zenger is guilty of libelling [making false statements about] his Excellency the Governor of New-York, and indeed the whole Administration of the Government. Mr. Hamilton has confessed the printing and publishing, and I think nothing is plainer, than that the words in the information are scandalous, and tend to sedition [inciting resistance to lawful authority] and to disquiet the minds of the people of this province. And if such papers are not libels, I think it may be said, there can be no such thing as a libel.

Mr. Hamilton: . . . the question before the court and you, gentlemen of the jury, is not of small nor private concern, it is not the cause of a poor printer, nor of New-York alone, which you are now trying; No! It may in its consequence, affect every freeman that lives under a British government on the main of America. It is the best cause. It is the cause of liberty; and I make no doubt but your upright conduct,

this day, will not only entitle you to the love and esteem of your fellow-citizens; but every man, who prefers freedom to a life of slavery, will bless and honour you, as men who have baffled the attempt of tyranny [oppressive power]; and by an impartial and uncorrupt verdict, have laid a noble foundation for securing to ourselves, our posterity [all future generations], and our neighbours, that to which nature and the laws of our country have given us a right— the liberty—both of exposing and opposing arbitrary power (in these parts of the world, at least) by speaking and writing truth. . . .

Mr. Chief Justice: Gentlemen of the jury. The great pains Mr. Hamilton has taken, to show how little regard juries are to pay to the opinion of the judges; and his insisting so much upon the conduct of some judges in trials of this kind; is done, no doubt, with a design that you should take but very little notice of what I may say upon this occasion. I shall therefore only observe to you that, as the facts or words in the information are confessed: the only thing that can come in question before you is, whether the words, as set forth in the information, make a libel. And that is a matter of law, no doubt, and which you may leave to the court. . . .

Zenger : The Jury withdrew, and in a small time returned, and being asked by the clerk, whether they were agreed of their verdict, and whether John Peter Zenger was guilty of printing and publishing libels in the information mentioned? They answered by Thomas Bunt, their Foreman, Not Guilty. Upon which there were three Huzzas [shouts of acclaim] in the hall which was crowded with people, and the next day I was discharged from my imprisonment.

Reprinted in: Colbert, David, ed. Eyewitness to America.

Andrew Hamilton (standing) defending John Peter Zenger during his trial. *Reproduced by permission of The Library of Congress.*

government was Richard Bradley, the attorney general (chief government law officer). In opening arguments at trial Hamilton pleaded that jury members were capable of deciding whether Zenger had printed truths or falsehoods, without guidance from presiding judge De Lancey. De Lancey denied this request, saying a judge is was more qualified to interpret the laws. Nevertheless, Hamilton proceeded to address his arguments directly to the jury.

When the time came to render the verdict, the jury ignored De Lancey's instructions. They concluded that Zenger's articles were based on fact, therefore finding him not guilty. The decision was cheered by spectators in the courtroom and later hailed by the general public. The verdict, which established the truth as a defense against libel charges, is considered the first significant victory for freedom of the press in America. The following year Zenger wrote a word-for-word account of the trial, which was published as *A Brief Narrative of the Case and Tryal of John Peter Zenger* (1736). His report was subsequently issued in several editions and generated considerable interest in the American colonies and in Britain.

In 1737 Zenger was appointed public printer for New York, and the next year he was awarded the same position in New Jersey. Although he had risen in his profession, he and his family continued to live in poverty. Zenger died in 1746, leaving his wife and six children. Anna Zenger published the *Journal* until December 1748. John Zenger, one of Zenger's sons from his first marriage, then managed the newspaper until it ceased publication in 1751.

For further research

Colbert, David, ed. *Eyewitness to America*. New York: Pantheon Books, 1997, pp. 41–44.

Krensky, Stephen. *The Printer's Apprentice*. New York: Bantam Doubleday Dell Books for Young Readers, 1996.

Putnam, William Lowell. *John Peter Zenger and the Fundamental Freedom*. Jefferson, N.C.: McFarland and Co., 1997.

Index

Italic type indicates volume numbers.

Bold type indicates main entries and their page numbers.

Illustrations are marked by (ill).